OLYMPIA
Cult, Sport, and Ancient Festival

OLYMPIA

CULT, SPORT, AND ANCIENT FESTIVAL

Ulrich Sinn

Translated from the German by
Thomas Thornton

 Markus Wiener Publishers
Princeton

THE TRANSLATION OF THIS BOOK INTO ENGLISH
WAS SUPPORTED BY A GRANT FROM INTER NATIONES

FOR INFORMATION WRITE TO: MARKUS WIENER PUBLISHERS
231 NASSAU STREET, PRINCETON, NJ 08542

BOOK DESIGN: CHERYL MIRKIN

LIBRARY OF CONGRESS CATALOGING-IN-PUBLICATION DATA

SINN, ULRICH
OLYMPIA: CULT, SPORT, AND ANCIENT FESTIVAL/ULRICH SINN;
TRANSLATED FROM GERMAN BY THOMAS THORNTON
INCLUDES BIBLIOGRAPHICAL REFERENCES AND INDEX.
ISBN 1-55876-239-6 HARDCOVER
ISBN 1-55876-240-X PAPER
1. OLYMPIC GAMES (ANCIENT)—HISTORY.
2. ARCHEOLOGY—GREECE.   I. TITLE.
GV23.S56 2000
306.4'83'0938—DC21   00-028275

MARKUS WIENER PUBLISHERS BOOKS ARE PRINTED IN THE
UNITED STATES OF AMERICA ON ACID-FREE PAPER,
AND MEET THE GUIDELINES FOR PERMANENCE AND DURABILITY
OF THE COMMITTEE ON PRODUCTION GUIDELINES FOR BOOK
LONGEVITY OF THE COUNCIL ON LIBRARY RESOURCES.

CONTENTS

ILLUSTRATIONS

INTRODUCTION

All Greeks had a lively interest in the Olympic competitions. In order to participate, the athletes, and hence the audience as well, had to travel to the west coast of the Peloponnesus, which is on the outskirts of the Greek motherland. Would a central location not have been more suitable for such an event?

We habitually gauge historical developments in ancient Greece by what happened in Athens, Corinth, or Sparta. Yet there was independent, self-confident life outside of these centers as well. Thus Olympia's rise to one of the supreme places of Greek culture is anything but odd or mysterious.

Initially, as a place of worship Olympia had doubtless no more than local significance. This book tries to sketch its development into the arguably most famous sanctuary in the Mediterranean. This is possible only if we let go of the assumption that Olympia was a stage for athletic competitions from the very start.

Admittedly, envisioning Olympia without athletes is not easy, as that is the location's aspect on which the ancient traditions center almost exclusively. Yet the Greeks did not begin to leave us written records until approximately seven centuries B.C., when the sanctuary was already four hundred years old. At that time the athletes had already entered the stage, and the memory of the location's relatively unspectacular early history had largely faded.

On our walk through Olympia's past we will at first use finds at the sanctuary as orientation points, no matter how insignificant they may seem. This will sharpen our eye for many hidden passages in the extant ancient sources, which will consequently reveal details about the local place of worship's early days.

The athletes were Olympia's main attraction. The popularity of its competitions was unequaled in ancient Greece, even leading in the fifth century B.C. to a vision of peace that could have decisively influenced Greek history—if human frailty had not quickly obliterated it.

Olympia itself emerged unharmed from this misfired attempt. During the next one thousand years the sacrarium kept changing its face. This transformation mirrored new philosophies of life, new trends in architecture, and improvements in technology.

The interest in continuing the old cult and its festival waned in the first half of the fifth century A.D. This did not mean, however, that the place, bustling with life until the end, was suddenly deserted. The former place of worship soon metamorphosed into a blossoming city whose history we can trace until the late sixth century A.D. The faithful now visited Olympia to attend services in a Christian church.

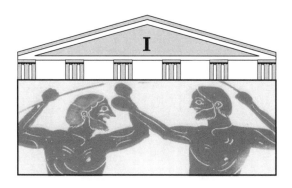

THE BATTLES FOR OLYMPIA

When the Olympic heralds began roaming through Greece to invite all citizens to the cult festival in the Zeus sanctuary, all hostilities ended, and all arms were laid down. The Greeks were allowed to enjoy the "divine peace" associated with the Olympic competitions. That was the picture of Olympia's special role that was painted in antiquity. In it Olympia appears to be the common property of all Greeks. This was but a dream image, an idea that did not adequately reflect harsh reality.

The territory inhabited by the Greeks never constituted a political community. It always consisted of many different autonomous regions (districts and city-states) that at best briefly formed larger alliances with others on occasion. Religion and—to a certain degree—language formed a common bond, but latent rivalries invariably led to discord and armed conflicts. This basic fact makes inconceivable an initiative of all Greeks to found and sustain a sanctuary together. No matter how many people would later be interested in the events at Olympia, this place of worship was originally established solely for one of the autonomous Greek districts and cultivated by its population.

The inhabitants of the district of Elis are mentioned in

Fig. 1. The Zeus sacrarium in the Alpheus valley with its rich vegetation.
The Hill of Cronus is on the left. The sanctuary was located in the plain before the hill's foot, extending with its arenas all the way to the wooded hills in the back. To the right is the Alpheus with the hills of Triphylia, whose inhabitants had once built the sanctuary.

almost every extant ancient document as the lords of the sanctuary. There can be no doubt that this is true from the early sixth century B.C. on—that historic fact was established by brute force. Originally Olympia was part of the district of Triphylia. Triphylia covered the area from the Alpheus valley in the north to the gorge of the Neda in the south. A stretch of sandy lagoons along the coast separates the inland, with its many lakes and brooks, from the ocean. That is where the legendary ruler Nestor resided. Homer, who was well familiar with the location, called it "sandy Pylos."

The name Triphylia means "land of the three tribes" or "land of the three districts." One of these districts included the Alpheus valley with the hilly country directly bordering it (see fig. 1). Its main city was Pisa, and the sanctuary of Olympia was nearby. That is why the Zeus sacrarium is sometimes poetically called Pisa in ancient literature.

Generally speaking, Triphylia was part of Arcadia. Therefore one can also simply state that until the early sixth century B.C., Olympia was supervised by Arcadia, but subsequently it came under Elis' sphere of influence.

Sources mention the controversy between the neighboring districts as far back as we can trace the history of the area in which Olympia was located. The oldest historic documents are the Homeric Poems, even though the name Olympia is not mentioned there. It was not the sanctuary that was the bone of contention, but its wider surroundings. The region's rich vegetation, which will be discussed in the following chapter, brought its inhabitants considerable wealth. Among those who profited from it was one of the great Homeric heroes: Nestor, ruler of Pylos. He owned a great deal of land south of the Alpheus. In the army camp before Troy he mentioned his constant conflicts with the cattle owners in the north of the Alpheus (*Iliad* 11, 670ff.).

By extending their sphere of influence to the fertile Alpheus valley in the early sixth century B.C., the Eleians automatically had control over the Zeus sacrarium. This was no pure joy for them at first. For a long time their reputation was tarnished because they had forcibly interfered with the tradition of the place of worship. Many of the Eleians' actions and decisions must be seen with this in mind. In the course of this book we will repeatedly discover consequences that were a direct outcome of this dilemma.

In the late fifth and early fourth century B.C. the pressure this put on them mounted. When the Spartans attacked Elis in the late fifth century B.C., the settlements conquered by the Eleians took advantage of the situation: with the aid of the victorious Spartans, they regained their independence. The issue of who was going to rule over the Zeus sanctuary was part of the capitulation negotiations between Sparta and Elis (Xenophon, *Hellenika* III 2, 21–31). The Eleians were forced to concede that Olympia had traditionally belonged to Triphylis. Yet they successfully argued that the Triphylians were only farmers and therefore incapable of taking charge of such an important site. For the time being the Zeus sacrarium remained under Elis' control.

Soon, however, the Eleians had to abandon their claim. After a long hiatus it was once again the original lords of the sanctuary who in 364 B.C. invited the Greek world to the cult festival. Seeing Olympia in the hands of the hateful Arcadians after all, the Eleians felt humiliated. They did not even shy away from attacking the sacrarium at the height of the cult festival, and advanced to the center of the shrine, the so-called Altis. Xenophon gives us a detailed description of the "Battle in the Altis" (*Hellenika* VII 4, 28–33). We will revisit this issue several times. At first the Eleians failed to win Olympia back; they did not manage to turn things around until several years later. From then on Olympia remained in Elis' hands for the remainder of its existence.

The Eleians' difficulties at justifying their claim to Olympia resulted in a development we ultimately have to view in a favorable light. Around 400 B.C., when the conflict with Arcadia (Triphylia) had come to a head, Elis commissioned the local scholar Hippias to write a chronicle of the sanctuary. The notes that had been kept on the victors in the competitions, which reached far back into the past, served Hippias as a guide for his history of the sacrarium. He produced a useful work that gained attention far beyond the borders of Elis. Subsequently the entire Greek world began to gradually base their calendar on the Olympic cult festivals.

Hippias' chronicle, however, did have a major shortcoming. There were no authentic notes available for the sacrarium's early years, before it became customary to leave written records, on which he could base his account of the champions. Yet that was probably just as well for Hippias and his employers, as it gave him room to skillfully invent certain facts that made Olympia's rise appear as Elis' accomplishment. According to Hippias, it was an Eleian king by the name of Iphitos who ages and ages ago, through a contract with the legendary Spartan lawgiver Lycurgus, had radically overhauled the competitions in Olympia, whose fame had spread beyond the local boundaries. His chronicle allowed Hippias also to distinguish Olympia in yet another respect: Iphitos and Lycurgus appear as the founders of the concept of Olympia as a symbol of peace and harmony among the Greeks by their proclaiming a divine peace (*ekecheiria*) for the duration of the cult festival.

This version of Olympia's early history gave the Eleians precisely what they so urgently needed: a purportedly historical document that legitimized their rule over the sacrarium in the eyes of the world. Yet the Eleians' intent was so obvious that Hippias' chronicle—at least its early passages—was recognized as bluntly bogus even in antiquity (Plutarch, *Lycurgus* 2 and 23, and *Numa* 1).

The year Hippias identified as the first Olympics organized by Elis, 776 B.C., has become a fixed date in Western historiography. In the course of this book we will see, however, that this does not mean that it constituted a caesura in the history of the sanctuary. At the end of chapter 8 we will also come to understand Hippias' probable method of reconstructing the history of the sacrarium.

As a result of the conflict over the Alpheus valley with its attractive sanctuary and the embellishment of historical truth by the Eleians, written historical records have painted an extremely lopsided picture of Olympia's beginnings. Still, despite Elis' attempts at mythologizing, we are able to trace the origins of the shrine.

The Greek Mainland

THE ORIGINS

"Olympia lies in the valley of the Alpheus, where the river runs through the territories of Pisatis and Triphylia. The whole country is full of temples of Artemis, Aphrodite, and the Nymphs, being situated in sacred precincts that are generally full of flowers because of the abundance of water." (Strabo VIII, 3,12.)

This description of the area according to Strabo is certainly an unfortunate introduction to Olympia if one intends to quickly get to the topic that gave the place its resounding name—the athletes' competitions, whose reputation was unique in the entire Greek world.

Yet this book will not introduce us to athletes or mention the tens of thousands flocking to Olympia to admire them for some time. First we will reconstruct more than three hundred years of the sanctuary's history, the period before Olympia became a place where athletic competitions took place—and no one can introduce us to that era better than Strabo.

Every sanctuary tends to preserve the intentions behind its foundation as expressed in the cult's own legends. Olympia is no exception. In this case, however, the collection of surviving sources does not help us much, for there exists a whole series of legends surrounding the foundation of this place of worship—

7

and the different accounts are not in agreement with each
other. In the previous chapter we have already discovered one
reason for this confusing inconsistency: it is the conflict over the
control of the sanctuary. Naturally, when the Eleians took
charge of the sacrarium, they bandied about a version that suited their purposes.

As we shall see, another reason for the different versions is
that in the course of the site's history Olympia's cult character
underwent repeated transformations. This happened with
other sanctuaries as well. It is not unusual for the legend of a
cult's foundation to be brought "up to date" after the cult has
taken on a new direction. The new version then reflected the
cult's new focus. Thus competitions take on a central role in
almost all Olympic cult legends. Characteristically, however,
there is also an entirely different version. We will take a closer
look at this in the following chapter.

Let us first ask ourselves how we can get to the historical
truth behind these confusing traditions. As paradoxical as it
sounds, even though more than three thousand years separate
us from the founding of Olympia, today we are better equipped
to comprehend the cult's beginnings than were the ancient historians, who were much closer to the events under consideration.

Someone from the Greece of the fifth century B.C. who was
interested in Olympia's early days had little to go by. The oldest
farmers were no longer alive, and many of the oblations from
the previous centuries had long since disappeared in the
ground. We, on the other hand, are familiar with these authentic documents of the early cult because they have gradually
been recovered through excavations begun in 1875. This constitutes a very revealing source aiding our attempt at discovering
the beginnings of the cult.

The active cult's earliest sources—a few jars from the latest
phase of Mycenian culture—date back to the eleventh century
B.C. During the tenth, ninth, and eighth centuries B.C. visitors
to the shrine usually offered miniature reproductions of ani-

mals as votive oblations. Thousands of these artifacts, which were made of clay or cast in bronze, were found in the course of the excavations. They are typically reproductions of cows and horses. Then there are also rams and dogs as well. The characteristic theme of Olympia's oblations is clearly cattle. Yet the farmers also produced images of themselves—naturally, in a particularly ostentatious way, as proud owners of wagons.

We find similar votive offerings in other, smaller sanctuaries in the surroundings of Olympia—for instance, in the Lapithus mountains south of Olympia, in a sanctuary of Artemis, where the goddess even had the telling epithet *Limnatis*, that is to say, "the one situated in the region abounding in water." Identical finds were made in an anonymous place of worship near the village of Mundritsa by the road to Andritsena. Again and again the theme is cattle, in other words, an agricultural population's assets. Therefore we are clearly led to see an inner connection between these votive oblations and the description of the region quoted at the beginning of this chapter.

Nestor, whom we encountered in chapter 1 as one of the landowners in the larger Olympia area, provides us with a corroboration of our assumption. The ruler of Pylos was downright raving as soon as he started talking about his herds of sheep and cows, or when he recalled his rich stock of "migrating goats." We also learn from him that there was serious horse breeding in the area as well.

Numerous descriptions from subsequent centuries confirm that the Homeric Hymns of the eighth century B.C. painted an accurate picture of Olympia's surroundings. Particularly revealing are the descriptions by Xenophon, who is known today as a friend of Socrates and as a participant in the campaign against the powerful Persian King Artaxerxes II. In the fourth century B.C. he farmed a large estate in Scillus near Olympia, a hilly land south of the Alpheus (see fig. 1). Xenophon celebrated the vast forests with their huge hunting grounds and was full of praise for the favorable conditions for agriculture and cattle breeding on his estate. Seen in this light, we imme-

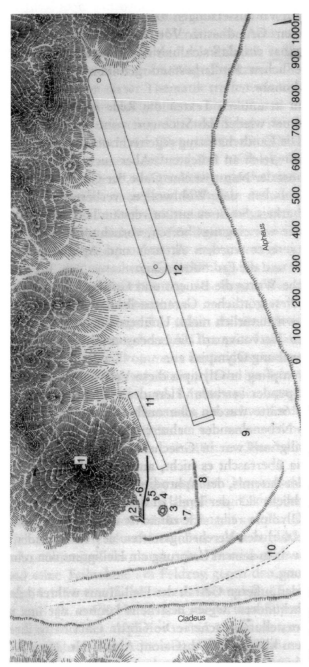

Fig. 2. The Zeus sanctuary in the early seventh century B.C.

From the time the sanctuary was founded around 1100 B.C., it centered around the Hill of Cronus (1), particularly its southern hillside, and this would last for more than the first four hundred years. The vegetation goddess Gaia was worshiped at the foot of the hill (2). The grave mound of Pelops (3) is among the oldest places of worship. Zeus did not receive a place of worship until the sanctuary was approximately one hundred years old. His altar (4) was also the site of an oracle. The latest research has cast doubt on the earlier assumption that the altars of Hera (5) and Hercules (6) were erected at the same time as Zeus'.

Around 700 B.C. the turbulent mountain brook Cladeus was redirected westward, behind a quay (10). The newly reclamated land was leveled and used for operating the sanctuary. A natural terrace (8) separated the sacred center from the bustling "festival meadow" (9). For the first time there was now enough room for building a stadium (11) and an aqueduct (12) in the east. When the Holy Olive Tree (7) was made a place of worship can no longer be precisely determined.

diately understand why the myth of Augeas with his stables full of countless cattle originated in this area.

All references to this region in ancient texts invariably mention its abundant harvests. The area was even called *eukarpus*, or "rich in crop." The sources also stress that being favored by nature is a gift from the gods. If they withdrew their favor, the land lost its fertility. Thus it is abundantly clear why it was predominantly vegetation gods that were worshiped in this area, as indicated earlier: Artemis and Aphrodite, but also Demeter and Earth Mother Gaia.

Obviously, we are not familiar with the content of the farmers and landowners' prayers to these guarantors of their prosperity. It is, however, evident that the animal votives allude to how the people in the area around Olympia lived.

Who received these votive offerings that were clearly made by farmers? The lord of the sanctuary was Zeus. Yet other gods were worshiped at the same site as well. It was not unusual in Greece to have several receptors of a cult within one sanctuary. That Olympia also had altars of the Earth Mother Gaia, of Artemis, Aphrodite, and Demeter, does not come as a surprise. Here is where the circle to the introductory quote closes. At first Olympia fit smugly into the many different places of worship in its surroundings. As a sanctuary it originally had strictly local significance.

We can only paint a vague picture of the external structure of the sanctuary during its first three centuries. The goddess Gaia had her altar on a small elevation (Gaion; fig. 2, no. 2) at the foot of the Hill of Cronus.

Around 700 B.C. the turbulent mountain brook Cladeus was redirected westward, behind a quay (fig. 2, no. 10). The newly reclamated land was leveled and used for operating the sanctuary. A natural terrace (no. 8) separated the sacred center from the bustling "festival meadow" (no. 9). For the first time there now was enough room for building a stadium (no. 11) and an aqueduct (no. 12) in the east. When the Holy Olive Tree (no. 7) was made a place of worship can no longer be precisely determined.

It is very likely that, even back then, the places of worship of Artemis and Aphrodite were right next to it, east of the Gaion. South of the Gaion, in the—at the time still rolling—plain there must have been a small grove in the direction of the Alpheus. Stands of trees were an integral part of Greek sanctuaries. The cult festivals' celebrations, for instance, took place there.

The altar of Zeus had its place in this grove (fig. 2, no. 4). Here is also where a knoll, covered with flat stones, was said to contain the grave of a hero from the distant past (fig. 2, no. 3). It was Pelops, whose rule purportedly began in Pisa, but whose activities and glory spread to Greece's entire southern peninsula, as a consequence of which it was named after him: Peloponnesus, or "Island of Pelops." We will have a closer look at that hero in a subsequent chapter.

Today we still cannot satisfactorily answer two questions regarding Olympia's early history. We are not sure precisely what parts Zeus and Gaia played in the very first phase of the sanctuary. Was Earth Mother Gaia temporarily the sole mistress of the sanctuary, before she had to surrender her position to Zeus after a span of perhaps no more than a few decades? A similar development took place in Apollo's sanctuary in Delphi, for instance. There the earth and oracle goddess Gaia was originally in the center of cultic worship, but later—approximately 1000 B.C.—she had to step aside to make room for Apollo.

We also lack firm knowledge on the course of the cult festival during the sanctuary's early period. There is no doubt that the inhabitants of the Alpheus Valley gathered regularly at the altars at the feet of the Hill of Cronus for celebrations.

We may also assume with certainty that they did not merely offer sacrifices and prayers but also enjoyed the general conviviality. Relishing communal meals, singing and dancing were integral parts of festive gatherings in honor of the gods since the days of old.

We can probably even take this thought one step further and also assume that competitions, too, were part of the earliest cult festivals. By consulting all extant news on early Greek cult festivals, we find numerous references to such competitions in a social setting. There could be first prizes for the grace of movements in dancing, musicians' performances, but of course also for all kinds of athletic interludes. If the traditions on Olympia make repeated references to races even in earliest times, we can no doubt take that at face value. In fact, it would be unusual if Olympia's visitors hadn't expressed their festive joy in that manner as well. We must, however, avoid one mistake: misunderstanding these races as specifically Olympian events. Rather, they constituted a convention of Greek cult festivals in general.

The votive offerings have helped us to get an idea of what made the inhabitants of the Alpheus Valley establish a place of worship on a hill on the border of that fertile region. Apparently they wanted to preserve nature's god-given blessings by giving thanks and making supplications regarding the future. To the natives, Zeus and the vegetation goddesses ensured the preservation of what their life depended upon.

Life in Greece with its autonomous regions, however, was determined by yet another worry. Latent conflicts among neighboring districts frequently led to hostilities. People believed that the decision about victory or defeat in battle was in the hands of the gods. Every battle was, therefore, preceded by offerings and prayers for a favorable outcome. This obviously also happened during the conflict among the inimical neighbors in the Alpheus Valley. We can once again turn to Nestor:

> Thence with all speed, arrayed in our armour, we came at midday to the sacred stream of Alpheus. There we sacrificed goodly victims to Zeus, supreme in might . . . when the bright sun stood above the earth we made prayer to Zeus and Athene, and joined battle.
>
> (Homer, *Iliad* XI 725–27 and 735–36)[1]

---

1. Ed. and tr. A. T. Murray, Loeb Classical Library 170 (Cambridge, Mass.: Harvard University Press, 1960; first printed in 1924).

Olympia also seems to have become a place of particular trust in the assistance from the gods in battles. In any event, the votive oblations indicate the arrival of new visitors to the sanctuary from the eighth century B.C. on.

THE ORACLE

Aside from votive offerings with clear agricultural references, other oblations were offered as well in Olympia from the eighth century B.C. on. They consisted of arms and armors made of bronze and iron. Elsewhere gods and goddesses also received armors and weapons from warriors. These offerings were often accompanied by the donor's thanks for returning unharmed from the battlefield. Naturally, warriors personally offered their thanks to the gods they felt particularly close to at their local sanctuary.

At the Zeus sanctuary in Olympia the situation is different. Arms and armors make up a major part of the finds at Olympia. Some of the armors came from many different regions in the Mediterranean, including several outside of Greece. A number of inscriptions, finally, leave no doubt about why they were dedicated: they were taken in battle. It must have been the cult of Olympia that made people offer such a vast number of armors and weapons at that sanctuary.

How can we reconcile the theme of war in Olympia's votive offerings and the idea of peace that originated from the place, as indicated in chapter 1? It has been customary among scholars to turn to Pausanias for clarification of this matter. Pausanias lived in the second century A.D. He has left us only

one work, but it is one of our richest sources in Greek culture.
Written in the form of a travelogue, it leads us to many important places on the Greek motherland. Pausanias skillfully
formed a succinct whole from what he saw, heard, and read. Of
particular value are his—generally precise—descriptions of
statues, buildings, and even entire sites, such as the Temple of
Zeus in Olympia. Without Pausanias' aid, the excavators would
have been able to identify but few of the sanctuary's buildings
and artifacts. Yet Pausanias has his weak spots too. It is fair to
say, for instance, that he had no understanding of historic inter-
connections and developments. Without any noticeable effort to
shed at least some light on the traditions, which were confusing
even in antiquity, he familiarizes us with different founding legends even he himself did not entirely comprehend. For an
understanding of Olympia's early history his work is not particularly helpful.

Strabo, whom we quoted earlier, had a quite different approach. He left us a multivolume work in which he gave us a
fair geographic description of the Mediterranean. It was written
in the early first century A.D., that is to say, during the reign of
Augustus. Since Strabo—and this is unusual for a topograph-
er—hardly traveled but gleaned almost his entire knowledge
from the pertinent literature, he certainly did not paint a historical picture of his period. What makes the chapter on Greece
particularly attractive is Strabo's enthusiasm for Homer. He
tried very hard to gain as precise an understanding as possible
from the entire literature available to him. Today we have come
to realize that the Homeric Hymns reflect the Greek world of
the eighth century B.C. That is the time into which Strabo leads
us when he walks in Homer's footsteps.

His research on Olympia's early history leads Strabo to a surprising conclusion: *At the outset the temple got fame on account
of the oracle of the Olympian Zeus.* Even though he does not
mention the word "war" in this context, Strabo does lead us into
the right direction in mentioning the oracle.

Aside from Strabo, another poet—who lived in the fifth cen-

Fig. 3. The sanctuary's center. Drawing by Friedrich Adler from 1894.
The Temple of Zeus, center, is surrounded by statues and very tall oblations. On the right is the ash altar of Zeus. The sacrificial fire was at the same time the site of the oracle. Zeus dispensed his advice on matters of war in the flames.

tury B.C. and has proven to be highly knowledgeable of Olympia as well—stressed Olympia's glorious history as the site of an oracle. We are talking about Pindar, who had the special gift of writing hymns of victory for athletic champions. These panegyrics always followed the same structural pattern: Pindar distributed praise equally on the victor and his family, on his hometown and, not least, on the sanctuary at whose festival the victory had been gained. He deftly interwove his poems with well-researched facts about important deeds and significant events in the pertinent families and places. Anyone interested in Olympia's earlier history will find the fourteen extant panegyrics on Olympic champions a veritable bonanza.

One of the victory hymns gives us the particular details of how the oracle at the foot of the Hill of Cronus was established: the god Apollo and Princess Euadne of Arcadia trysted in the reeds of the bank of the Alpheus, which are very difficult to access. As a result of their union, Euadne, concealed in the reeds, gave birth to a boy who was named Iamus. Snakes fed the child, who remained hidden at the foot of the Hill of Cronus. It took some time for Apollo to remember his son, who he then decided should get the best education possible. He brought him to his place in Delphi, where he taught him the art of prophecy, and established a site at the place where he was born so he could practice his skill. Apollo and his half-brother Hercules prepared the ground and dedicated the newly erected temple to their common father Zeus. Iamos and his sons after him, the Iamids, read the signs sent by Zeus in the flames of the sacrificial fire (fig. 3). Later on the Iamids were joined by the offspring of another great seer by the name of Clytius, the Clytiads.

For a long time the fairy tale about the Arcadian princess, the god, and the ultimately happy ending of their romance were not seriously taken into account when analyzing the history of the sanctuary.

Yet where do we find the news on an oracle at the altar of Zeus Olympius? Among the voluminous traditions on Olympia only two brief episodes refer to a consultation with the oracle. In the fourth century B.C. a legation from Sparta inquired of the oracle of the Olympian Zeus about the permissibility of the city-state's battle against the city of Argos. A few decades earlier, back in the fifth century B.C., the Spartan King Agis' attempt to make use of the Olympian seer's wisdom failed, because Iamus' offspring refused to divulge any information on the outcome of a war for which the king had made preparations.

At second glance these two inquiries, which are historically documented, are not really as isolated as they first appear to be. Again a reading of Pindar's panegyrics leads us onto an interesting track. Pindar not only tells us the story behind the foundation of the oracle. At the same time he also testifies to the high art of Olympia's lineage of seers: Pindar tells us that when the Greeks set out to found colonies in Lower Italy and Sicily, they were accompanied in their dangerous undertaking—necessarily involving armed conflict—by a member of Olympia's family of seers. It was his advice that made them prevail in their endeavor to settle in Syracuse, as strangers in a foreign land.

Two aspects in Pindar's report make us sit up. One, this third mention of the Olympian oracle contains for the third time the advice in a military matter. Two, the people seeking the advice do not approach the oracle; rather, the seer rushes to the place where his advice is needed: the battlefield. Evidently the Olympian seers did not operate exclusively at their own oracle site.

Once we have become aware of this peculiarity, we suddenly begin to notice a number of things we did not expect. Hardly any of the memorable battles in Greek history were fought without the presence of an Iamid or a Clytiad, that is to say, without the aid of an Olympian seer. The defeat of the Persians on the battlefield of Plataea in 479 B.C. must be credited to the Olympian seer, as must the decisive battle of Aeguspotamoi, which in 405 B.C., after almost thirty years of war between Sparta and Athens, finally brought the Spartans victory. The

Olympian makers of oracles were once memorably called "field clergymen."

Even though the Iamids and Clyatids hardly ever worked in Olympia itself, their success elsewhere clearly left its mark on the sanctuary. Keeping in mind the Olympian seers' evident specialization on advice in matters of war, we also begin to understand why no other archaeological excavation on Greek soil uncovered as many arms and armors as the ones at the sanctuary of Zeus at Olympia.

Yet this collection of oblations—impressive in itself—contains other items as well: there are countless statues and buildings that were erected for the Olympian Zeus for the same purpose. In the course of their history, many Greek cities in the motherland as well as the colonies immortalized a military victory by dedicating a victory monument in Olympia to the god who had brought it about.

The most famous monument of this kind is the statue of Nike, financed by the Messenians from war booty, which stands in front of the Zeus temple on a thirty-foot pillar (fig. 3, far left). This monument, which has been largely restored, marks the area of the sanctuary that was once covered with similarly lavish trophies and war monuments. Since it was customary to offer to the god who had brought the victory one-tenth of all war booty as thanks, a monument's external appearance indicated the degree of success that had been granted in battle—if everyone followed the custom. But who could have withstood the temptation of making one's victory shine even more brightly by erecting a more magnificent statue? Thus the cities kept competing with each other in displaying the splendor of their monuments. Among them were numerous colossal figures of double or even triple life-size. The bronze statue of Zeus the Eleians erected in the 360s B.C. after the victory they had won with great difficulty over the Arcadians (see chapter 1) reached a size of thirty feet.

Another votive genre characteristic of the early Olympian period also belongs among the oblations offered after successful battles. These are the bronze kettles on three legs that were used especially in the ninth and eighth centuries B.C. At home this kind of houseware was typically used for heating liquids on a stove. Yet these "tripod kettles" offered at Olympia were not taken from the households of their donors. We can conclude from their often rich artistic ornaments that they were specially crafted as precious oblations. Furthermore, their typically oversize dimensions made them unfeasible for use at home. The largest samples reached a staggering height of ten feet. These precious tripod kettles found widespread use in the Greece of the ninth and eighth centuries B.C. Once again Olympia turns out to be a site richer in these oblations than any other place.

For a long time scholars were convinced they knew the reason for the tripod offerings, as the victors in chariot races described by Homer received such tripods as victory prizes (*Iliad* XI 700 and XXIII 264). That seemed to fit perfectly into Olympia's role as a venue. A careful analysis of all sites where such tripods were found, however, as well as a thorough reading of ancient texts, tells us that the samples found in Olympia are by no means proof that chariot races took place there as early as the ninth and eighth centuries B.C. Rather, along with a wide variety of other elaborate and precious metal vessels, the tripods found constituted representative offerings on different occasions during that time period. For instance, we read about them as popular xenial presents in the Homeric Hymns (*Iliad* IX 122; *Odyssey* IV 129, XIII 13, XV 84; see also Plutarch, *Solon* 4). The Greek army commander Agamemnon, on the other hand, promised them to his fellow warriors as a thank-offering in case of a victory in Troy (*Iliad* VII 290). Thus the tripods were also suitable for giving thanks to the Olympian oracle.

Among all these thank-offerings Zeus received as the lord of the war oracle, one deserves closer attention, as it looked strange to Greeks. These are the arms and armors the Greeks, who had emigrated to the Italian peninsula in the late eighth century B.C., had taken as booty in battles with the local population. After successfully colonizing the area, they evidently visited the sanctuary—Pindar reports that its seer had aided them in their daring enterprise—to offer their thanks, giving Zeus his share of their war booty. This marked the beginning of a particularly close bond between the colonizers of Lower Italy and the Zeus sanctuary.

The enhanced reputation this entailed for Olympia signified the most crucial caesura at the turn from the eighth to the seventh century in Olympia's long history.

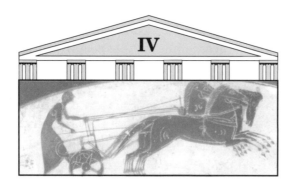

COMING HOME
FOR THE OLYMPICS

The stupendous success of the Olympian seers in the colonialists' retinue brought Olympia more than just oblations. The sanctuary also took on a new role: it became the preferred meeting point of émigré Greeks and their fellow tribesmen who had remained at home. From now on they held their cult celebrations together in the Alpheus Valley.

Naturally, dealing with this vastly increased influx of participants was possible only by expanding the sanctuary. Indeed, excavations of recent years have brought to light clear proof of efforts in that direction. As described earlier, until the late eighth century B.C. the sanctuary was basically confined to the south side of the Cronus Hill and a small area in the adjacent plain stretching southward toward the Alpheus. The area west of the Cronus Hill and the Gaion could not be used, as the bed of the Cladeus was located there, an at times torrential mountain brook that could seriously flood the area, especially of course in the wintertime. The area to the south and southeast of the Cronus Hill was so uneven that its potential use for the sanctuary's purposes was strictly limited.

That did not change until around 700 B.C., when the ground approximately in the section today's visitors see (see fig. 2) was moved and the area leveled. Naturally, making the western part of the place accessible was especially difficult, as this involved redirecting the Cladeus. The river had to be tamed by way of a protecting wall (fig. 2, no. 10) lest it exercise its ferocious power in the wintertime. Today remnants of an ancient quay can be seen on the west bank of the Cladeus (though what we see is the inner side of the wall, as the riverbed was obviously west of this barrier!).

More recent excavations brought to light proof not only of the tremendous size of the sacred area. The need to provide for a significantly larger number of visitors from approximately 700 B.C. on also left its distinct archaeological traces. Suddenly there were insufficient water supplies to accommodate all of the pilgrims. This led to the custom—also around 700 B.C.—of digging deep wells into the sandy ground for the duration of the cult festival, which allowed the Olympians access to the abundant groundwater that was available twelve to twenty feet underground. We will return to the methods of obtaining water in chapter 13.

Pindar and Strabo, our two sources on Olympia's early history, both describe the extraordinary splendor of the cult festival. The Greeks called it *panegyris*, literally "festive assembly of the entire people." Its highlight was of course the sacred ceremonies. Still, the Greek term's connotations of a public festival with all its accompanying enjoyable activities reveal the true nature of these events. Conviviality with abundant food and drink, conversations, song, and dance constituted the main attraction of Greek cult festivals.

The specific way these celebrations took place certainly made it a marvelous opportunity for many to spend time with people they otherwise never saw. The Olympian *panegyris'* particular appeal was the presence of many Greeks from the colonial cities in Lower Italy ("Greater Greece," "Western Greece").

There are many different indications for Olympia's role as the place where expatriate Greeks met on a regular basis. An unusually large percentage of oblations was donated by such expatriate Greeks. The group of so-called treasury houses (or treasuries) at the foot of the Cronus Hill (fig. 9, no. 6) can serve as a good example. At least eight of the eleven temple-like, particularly precious monuments were donated by colonial cities.

We can probably also attribute to the western colonies the fact that among the finds at Olympia is a surprisingly large number of household utensils and artifacts from Etruria. Among them are not only genuinely Etruscan objects but probably also the numerous Oriental-style items made of metal that were offered in Olympia—for many Phoenician artists worked in Etruria, a territory rich in metals. When Greeks from beyond the Adriatic Sea came to the Olympian festival, they apparently liked to bring as oblations items in the much-admired Oriental style. This allowed them to give their friends in the motherland a taste of their new home.

The tremendous accumulation of oblations, and not least their considerable material and artistic value, entailed the need for buildings in which these offerings could be housed safely and in a worthy manner. In approximately the mid-seventh century the first treasuries were built in Olympia. None of their architecture has survived, since the building materials—wood and clay—decayed over time. Only the bronze reliefs that once decorated the white-washed walls attest to their existence. These first treasure houses were probably situated on the terraced southern side of the Hill of Cronus (fig. 2, east of no. 6), at the place where the stone buildings housing the oblations were located as well.

Its many festival attendants "from overseas" made Olympia attractive to a group of people whose frequent presence at the sanctuary was not always religiously motivated.

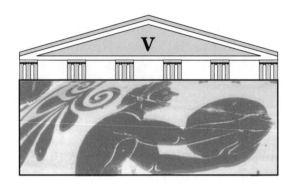

THE ATHLETES

When around 700 B.C. the sacred area was expanded to accommodate the ever increasing influx of people, the ground was leveled in the eastern part of the new area as preparation for the construction of running tracks (fig. 2, no. 11). This stadium—the earliest one discovered at Olympia—was located approximately at the site of the later, larger Stadium, which we can view today in its reconstructed form (fig. 12). South of the stadium the Hippodrome was built probably not much later (fig. 2, no. 12).

It is of course no coincidence that the expansion of the cult festival and the installation of venues occurred at the same time. Naturally the festival-goers who had come from far away expected an interesting and entertaining program around the *panegyris*. From the athletes' point of view, too, the "new Olympia" with its more than local *panegyris* was now becoming really interesting: those who made it there quickly became famous in all the cities from where visitors were now pouring into Olympia, not least in all overseas colonies.

Sources document this particular motivation for people involved in the cult festival in different capacities: artists and scholars went to Olympia to present their works and ideas because they wanted to publicize them throughout the Greek world. We know of a very specific example—the historian Herodotus, who wrote his works in the fifth century B.C.:

> As soon as he sailed from his home in Caria straight for Greece, he bethought himself of the quickest and least troublesome path to fame and a reputation for both himself and his works. To travel round reading his works, now in Athens, now in Corinth or Argos or Lacedaemon in turn, he thought a long and tedious undertaking that would waste much time. The division of his task and the consequent delay in the gradual acquisition of a reputation did not appeal to him, and he formed the plan of winning the hearts of all the Greeks at once somewhere if he could. The great Olympian games were at hand, and Herodotus thought this the opportunity he had been hoping for. He waited for a packed audience to assemble, one containing the most eminent men from all Greece; he appeared in the temple chamber, presenting himself as a competitor for an Olympic honor, not as a spectator; then he recited his *Histories* and so bewitched his audience that his books were called after the Muses, for they too were nine in number. By this time he was much better known than the Olympic victors themselves. There was no one who had not heard the name of Herodotus—some at Olympia itself, others from those who brought the story back from the festival.
>
> (Lucian, *Aëtion* 1–2[1])

We may safely assume that Olympia's sudden rise to the most popular venue in Greece can be attributed to very similar ideas on the part of the athletes.

We saw in chapter 2 that athletic contests probably took place even during the first centuries of Olympia's existence, that is to say, between the eleventh and eighth centuries B.C. One gets the impression that even Hippias' list of champions, which was fabricated for Olympia's early days (see chapter 1), reflects such an unspectacular prelude to the Olympic contests that later became such large, celebrated events. After all,

---

1. *Lucian VI*, tr. K. Kilburn, Loeb Classical Library 430 (Cambridge, Mass.: Harvard University Press, 1990; first printed in 1959), pp. 145–47.

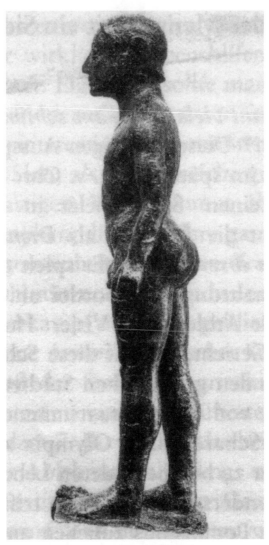

Fig. 4. Bronze figurine of athlete from around 500 B.C., discovered at Olympia.
In the sixth century B.C. it became customary for victorious athletes to
express their thanks in the form of statuettes. Naturally, these dedications
were in part an expression of the Olympic champions' pride. To keep this kind
of self-promotion from turning into unbridled vanity, the sanctuary administra-
tration issued strict rules concerning the figurines' size. The athletes were
always able to commission the best sculptors of their day. Unfortunately, none
of these works has survived. The above miniature figurine, a little over 4.5
inches tall, has the standard format of a sixth-century victor's statuette.
Perhaps it was dedicated before a contest as a prayer offering by an athlete.

Hippias starts out by mentioning only simple races, and he only mentions victors from Olympia's proximity. Contests in the prominent heavy athletic disciplines and chariot races appear only much later in his catalog of champions. During Olympia's first few centuries, athletic contests—if indeed there were any—took place on the fringes of the cult activities.

Yet it was not only the contests whose character changed during that period. The participants themselves also underwent a transformation. We have to let go of the notion that athletic contestants at a cult festival were from the circle of regular sanctuary visitors. As early as the seventh century B.C. they constituted a clearly defined group of specialists who stood outside the everyday life of their native communities, and who focused exclusively on their appearances at any of the numerous contests taking place as part of Greek cult festivals (fig. 4). Already voices could be heard that were highly critical of the new class of athletes.

THE OLYMPIC COMPETITION

Even though not every piece of information on the early Olympic competitions is verifiable, we do know for certain that the Zeus sanctuary attracted the best athletes of their day for the astonishingly long period of altogether more than one thousand years. This is all the more baffling as in almost all other areas of Greek culture and society, quite significant changes took place between 700 B.C. and A.D. 400. Thus participation in the contests was limited almost exclusively to the members of the nobility, the *aristocrats*, until the fourth century B.C., when they lost their privileges to a large middle class. In the wake of that development, although athletes with a less distinguished background began to compete at Olympia, the athletic contests still lost none of their attraction.

The Olympic festival survived the collapse of the old political structures unscathed as well: as late as the fifth century B.C., what city an athlete came from was crucially important. At that time Greece comprised a territory that was subdivided into hundreds of autonomous city-states. Competing at Olympia invariably also meant establishing the strength and power of an athlete's hometown. Consequently, victorious athletes were richly rewarded at home (see pages 47–8). Competition among the cities was one of the main motives for the struggle for Olympic laurels. Nonetheless, neither the political restructuring of the country since Alexander the Great (336–323 B.C.) nor the incorporation of Greece into the Roman Empire (since 148 B.C.) could diminish the glory of the Olympic festival.

What is probably most astonishing is a fact most recent excavations have revealed: that the Olympic contests survived unscathed even in the midst of the religious confusion during the fourth and continuing into the fifth century A.D. (see chapter 18).

One of the probable reasons for this singular success was that throughout all of the centuries of Olympia's function as a venue, the athletic contests strictly followed the old Olympic tradition. It is not only today that people tend to yearn for the "good old days"—in antiquity, too, that longing was widespread. For many, the Olympic contests with their old and rich tradition seems to have embodied these "good old days," which is why they were carefully and meticulously preserved.

Let us now take a look at the individual athletic events that were part of the Olympic program, which during the several centuries of Olympia's existence underwent only insignificant changes in the way they were held. Most attempts at expanding the athletic program were dropped very quickly. Thus the inscription on a plaque that was recently discovered, with the names of Olympic champions from the fourth century, reveals nothing that had not existed during the previous centuries as well (see fig. 20).

RUNNING

According to ancient tradition, running was the oldest Olympic event. An indication for its distinctive status is that the period of four years following the festival, the so-called Olympiad, was named after the champion in the simple foot race.

There were three running contests. The track in Olympia's Stadium was six hundred feet long—in today's measurements,

Fig. 5. Bronze figurine found at Olympia of a runner about to start a race, from around 490 B.C.

Runners started in a standing position. Deep indentations for the toes in the stone starting marks served as footholds. False starts were largely prevented by opening barriers in front of the runners simultaneously. Punishment for early starts was flogging.

roughly 210 yards. Nowhere else did runners have to cover such a great distance. At contests in honor of Apollo on the isle of Delos, runners reached the finishing line after only 182.6 yards. The reason for the different track lengths lies in the above-mentioned autonomy of Greek city-states. Each territory had its own measurements. Thus one stade equaled six hundred feet in each city, but the actual distance depended on the length of a foot, which varied from place to place. At 12.8 inches, it was particularly long in Olympia. Since what was measured in antiquity was not the time it took to finish a race—all that counted was who came in first—the differences in linear measures did not matter. Obviously, that conditions were especially tough at Olympia was common knowledge. Accordingly, a victory at an Olympic foot race was viewed with very special regard.

Runners were not only barefoot, they were completely naked (see pages 34–5). The runners' starting positions were drawn by lot. The contestants started standing, leaning slightly forward, with their arms almost horizontally stretched out in front (fig. 5). Some stadiums had sophisticated starting machines with barriers that could be lowered. They were released at the same time for all athletes. Generally, however, the problem of false starts was limited by the threat of flogging.

In addition to the simple foot race, there was also a double-course contest. This version was called *díaulus*. At the end of the lap each runner had to make a sharp turn and run back to the starting line. We know this form of racing back and forth from today's swimming competitions. A third running contest was the *dólikhus*, in which the runners had to race through the stadium twenty times. In Olympia, this equaled a distance of a little over 4,150 yards, or 2.36 miles.

We all know that the famous marathon goes back to an event in Greek antiquity: an Athenian messenger is said to have run the roughly twenty-six miles between Marathon and Athens in 490 B.C. to inform his fellow citizens that, against all expectations, Athens' army had put the overpowering Persian armed force to flight. Yet there was no equivalent to today's marathon either at Olympia or as part of any other athletic competition in any Greek city.

In the late sixth century, the combination of sports and military needs led to an additional Olympic event in a different way: runners now competed in full armor. Since by that time more foot soldiers were employed in war than before, this contest simultaneously served as military training. Yet the introduction of this discipline was probably also a response to those critics who claimed that Olympic sports were detrimental to the cities' ability to defend themselves (see chapter 7). That it was ultimately indeed more a symbolic combination of sport and military concerns becomes blatantly clear when we consider that the armor of the so-called armed runners was limited to helmet and shield. Otherwise they were unclothed, just like other runners.

THE ATHLETES' NUDITY

Why did the runners and, with the exception of the charioteers, all other athletes compete in the nude? This question was raised even back in antiquity—only to receive quite different answers.

An important source is the historical oeuvre of *Thucydides*, who wrote in his review of early Greek history:

> An unpretentious costume after the present fashion was first adopted by the Lacedaemonians. . . . And they were the first to bare their bodies and, after stripping openly, to anoint themselves with oil when they engaged in athletic exercise; for in early times, even in the Olympic games, the athletes wore girdles about their loins in the contests, and it is not many years since the practice has ceased. Indeed, even now among some of the Barbarians, especially those of Asia, where prizes for wrestling and boxing are offered, the contestants wear loin-cloths.
>
> (Thucydides I 6[1])

1. *History of the Peloponnesian War*, with an English translation by Charles Forster Smith, vol. 1, Loeb Classical Library 108 (Cambridge, Mass.: Harvard University Press, 1991; 1st revised edition printed in 1928), pp. 13–15.

Unfortunately, we cannot attach specific dates to Thucydides' general statement, "It was not long ago," since in that part of his history, the author covers Greece's mythic prehistoric times, for which there is no concrete time frame.

The story the writer Pausanias adopted in the second century A.D. from older sources is more helpful: "Near Coroebus is buried Orsippus, who won the foot-race at Olympia by running naked when all his competitors wore girdles according to ancient custom." (Pausanias I 44, 1[2]) Pausanias' comment on this piece of information is interesting, as it shows that even in his day, people wondered why the athletes competed in the nude: "My own opinion is that at Olympia he intentionally let the girdle slip off him, realizing that a naked man can run more easily than one girt."

We notice that the ancient explanations for the athletes' nudity were highly pragmatic. This indicates that Greek culture was generally not at all self-conscious about any issues concerning the human body, sexuality, and eroticism.

WRESTLING

Greek wrestling required a tremendously well-balanced combination of strength and skill. In the twenty-third book of his *Iliad*, the poet Homer describes a typical wrestling match during the eighth century B.C. The opponents are of course the two famous Greek princes Odysseus and Ajax. The match ended in a draw, since Ajax was superior in physical strength, but Odysseus managed to avoid defeat owing to his nimble mind and body.

In order to win the victor's crown, a contestant had to throw his opponent three times, with the loser's shoulders touching the ground. Thus a match could have a maximum of five rounds, if the result was three to two. The victor's glory—and accordingly, the excitement in the arena—was infinitely greater

---

2. *Description of Greece*, vol. 1, tr. W. H. S. Jones, Loeb Classical Library 93 (Cambridge, Mass.: Harvard University Press, 1993; first published in 1918), p. 237.

if one of the wrestlers managed to avoid being thrown even once. Such a victory "without touching the ground" made for a particularly honorable entry into the annals of history.

Among the combatant sports, wrestling was no doubt the least rough, even though attacks against the entire body, including kicks, were permitted. Punishment for violations of the contest rules was severe. For instance, if a fighter deliberately broke his opponent's fingers, he had to pay a huge fine and was flogged.

BOXING

It is documented that boxing existed even during the Minoan-Mycenean era of the second century B.C. Again it is Homer who described for us a boxing match that took place during the early years of Greek history:

> So the twain, when they had girded themselves, stepped into the midst of the place of gathering, and lifting their mighty hands on high one against the other, fell to, and their hands clashed together in heavy blows. Dread was the grinding of their teeth, and the sweat flowed on every side from off their limbs. But upon him goodly Epeius rushed as he peered for an opening, and smote him on the cheek, nor after that, methinks, did he long stand upright, for even there did his glorious limbs sink beneath him. . . . his dear comrades thronged about him and led him through the place of gathering with trailing feet, spitting out clotted blood and letting his head hang to one side. . . .
>
> (Homer, *Iliad* XXIII 686–98, excerpts[3])

The boxers' equipment included leather straps (*himántes*) that were wrapped around the fighter's forearms from the elbows to the fingers, with the fingertips remaining uncovered. On the one hand these bandages served to stabilize the wrists. On the other they were used to deliberately injure one's oppo-

---

3. Tr. A T. Murray, Loeb Classical Library 170 (Cambridge, Mass.: Harvard University Press, 1960; first printed in 1924), pp. 545–47.

Fig. 6. Amphora from around 530 B.C. depicting a boxing match.
The two muscular boxers are on the attack, their arms raised. They are thus following a rule that is difficult to understand from today's point of view: all punches had to be directed at the opponent's head. More than a few boxers were knocked unconscious. It is documented that some even died. Admiration for outstanding athletic accomplishments was so great that numerous athletes became the objects of cultic worship: they were elevated into *heroes* (demigods). It is telling that the list of athletes thus honored contains almost exclusively the names of heavy athletes.

nent. This was done mainly by cutting the hard leather strap, which was almost one centimeter thick, to sharpen its edges, and eventually even inserting metal pieces.

The luck of the draw decided who one's opponent was. The fighters approached each other with raised arms. The contest rules prohibited clinching the opponent's body. Hard as it may be to believe, the ancient rules stipulated that all punches had to be directed at the opponent's head. We have already seen that this is how Epeius gained his victory in Homer's description quoted above.

As harsh as this sport was, boxing could also be downright comical at times: if a boxer had significantly shorter arms than his opponent, he obviously had no chance of landing a blow at the other fighter's head. Thus it is said to have occurred that an athlete with long arms kept them stretched out to let his opponent "starve," much to the amusement of the spectators. Still, stories like this must not blind us to the fact that many matches were fights for life and death, which provided just the kind of drama the fans thirsted for. While the contest rules specified that each match could be stopped through precisely defined shouts or signs, avoiding an impending knockout was considered disgraceful. It is no coincidence that the most famous Olympic victors of antiquity are to be found among the boxers (see chapter 7). Still, when it comes to the brutality of fighting, boxing was surpassed by yet another discipline:

THE PANKRATION

The list of combatant sports is concluded by, and culminates in, the *pankration*. Literally translated, the word means "all-fight." It combined the essential possibilities and specific challenges of wrestling and boxing, without the leather straps of boxing but strangleholds being permissible. Only biting and moves for the opponent's eyes are documented to have been prohibited. Matches always started from a standing position. As a rule they ended with the opponents in a wrestling clinch on the floor. Several sources mention that athletes tried to strangle their opponents. In order to stay alive, the athlete in need could signal for the fight to be stopped by raising his hand with one or three fingers stretched out. Yet when an athlete ended a match in this manner, the spectators responded with indignation and derision. More than a few pankration fighters died in the arena.

A man by the name of Arrhakhion from the town of Phigalia in Arcadia won especial fame. The following story about his appearance at Olympia made history: Arrhakhion was already a two-time Olympic pankration champion when he came up against a younger and stronger opponent during his third Olympic Games. Still, he tried everything in his power to gain the highest glory an athlete could win: being a three-time Olympic champion. When after a long fight he was inescapably trapped in his opponent's stranglehold and was facing death, he once again gathered all the strength he had left to not leave this life peacefully. He had just enough left in him to pinch the young athlete hard in the foot. At that moment two sounds could be heard in Olympia's Stadium: Arrhakhion's last breath and his opponent's whining outcry. To the spectators' thundering applause, the umpires declared Arrhakhion the—posthumous!—victor. . . . He was the kind of man people wanted to receive the Olympic victor's laurel wreath.

It could also happen that a contestant was declared the winner of a pankration match without him having actually fought: when word got around that a particularly good fighter had entered the Olympic contest, others, who had now lost their hopes of winning the championship, would withdraw on occasion to avoid the disgrace of losing in the Stadium.

THE PENTATHLON

The Greek pentathlon included discus, long jump, javelin, running, and wrestling. As we have seen, running and wrestling also existed as individual events. Long jump, discus, and javelin events, however, were held only as part of the pentathlon.

Fig. 7. Two categories of the pentathlon. Scene on an amphora from the late sixth century B.C.
On the far left a discus thrower is in the starting position: he will now bend further forward to gain momentum for his throw by making the twisting motion characteristic of this sport. The two other athletes lead us to the long jump. The long jumper (right) can be recognized from the hangerlike weights (*haltéres*) in his hands. As long as the musician next to him plays a melody of predetermined length on the oboe (*aulus*), the athlete, who starts in a standing position, can make one jump after another. From his posture we can see that he has just landed after one of these jumps.

There were several perplexing peculiarities to the pentathlon. The way it was set up, it was really a triathlon that could be expanded by two additional rounds if necessary. In other words, all those who had entered the pentathlon competition competed only in the first three disciplines—discus, long jump, and javelin. After completion of the javelin, the results were added up. If one and the same athlete had won in all three categories, he was immediately declared champion in the "pent"athlon!

However, if no winner had been determined yet, only those leading the competition were admitted to the fourth event. They then entered the running contest. Afterward it was again determined if one of the athletes had already surpassed all the others. If that was again not the case, the decision was indeed made after the fifth contest, wrestling.

There has been much debate among researchers on the technical execution of the individual disciplines. While ancient literary and artistic sources have supplied us with a great deal of information, they do not always suffice to provide us with enough details that would allow us to reliably reconstruct the actual particulars of the contest.

LONG JUMP

In this regard the long jump is the most confusing event. We know that long jumpers used hanger-like weights (fig. 7, right). These "jumping weights" (*haltére*) weighed up to more than five pounds, depending on their size. Obviously, with two such weights in their hands, the athletes were unable to sprint during the approach run. On the other hand, we are told that they achieved enormous distances. A Spartan athlete by the name of *Chionis* is said to have jumped fifty-two Olympic feet (or 53.65 feet). Another athlete supposedly jumped 53.4 feet in Delphi. Careful analysis of all written sources from antiquity suggests that the ancient long jumpers made several standing jumps in a row within a given time period. This technique allowed the jumping weights, which were swung forward, to increase the

jumper's forward momentum considerably. Actual experiments
have shown that with five such standing jumps one can indeed
reach distances of more than fifty feet. To prevent the athletes
from pausing between individual jumps as long as they wished
and instead force them to make several jumps in a row, a
melody played by an oboe (*aulus*, fig. 7, center) made sure that
each participant made a sequence of jumps within the same
time frame.

Like all the other pentathlon events, the long jump took place
in the Stadium. Before the contest, the ground in the jumping
area was loosened up with picks. Since excavations brought to
light jumping weights—typically made of stone—of quite different shape and size, it is not impossible that the athletes were
allowed to choose their own personal jumping weights. An athlete who chose a heavy weight could thus increase his forward
momentum, but on the other hand, this also increased gravity's
downward pull. In any case, the advantages and disadvantages
were balanced, so that the athletes' individual choice did not
create unfair conditions.

JAVELIN THROWING

Javelin throwing, too, had a peculiarity: a thin leather strap
was wrapped approximately around the middle of the shaft of
the javelin. The end of the strap formed a noose (*ankyle*) into
which the javelin thrower put his index and middle fingers just
as he was about to throw the javelin. As soon as it was released,
the wrapping came undone at lightning speed, which resulted
in a twisting motion of the javelin. By quickly turning around
its own axis, the javelin's flight was stabilized and lasted longer,
which resulted in greater distances.

Javelin throwing in the small stadium was not without its
dangers for the spectators. If an athlete threw the javelin diagonally to the Stadium axis and the javelin landed outside the
track, an accident was inevitable. Indeed it seems that this happened on occasion.

DISCUS THROWING

According to all the information on discus throwing we can glean from ancient texts and visual depictions, this discipline's technique was essentially the same as is standard today. There are significant differences in size and weight of the discuses—typically made of bronze—that were unearthed during excavations. The flat discs had diameters of between 42.5 and 85 inches, and weights of between 3.3 and 14.3 pounds. Contestants at the same event did, of course, use discuses of the same size and weight (fig. 7, left).

Running and wrestling followed the same rules that applied to the individual events.

CHARIOT RACES AND HORSE RACING

The tradition of chariot races is not only especially old—in Greece as well as many of its neighboring countries it was also considered the most distinguished athletic event. That it was practiced at Olympia for the first time in the seventh century, proves once more that Olympia did not become a venue for athletic contests until relatively late (see chapter 5).

Contrary to many athletic events that in the course of the country's historic development became accessible to a broader spectrum of Greek society, chariot races always remained in the domain of aristocrats and the prosperous. The reason for this was in the considerable expense involved in horse breeding. There is another peculiarity that distinguished chariot races from other sports: the winner of a race was not the chariot driver, on whose skill and daring the outcome of the race depended. The glory of being an Olympic champion was always bestowed on the owner of the horses, who did not even have to be present at the Olympic Games. This explains why statesmen, military commanders, and eventually even Roman emperors could adorn themselves with the title of Olympic Champion (see chapter 7). It logically follows that even women could win chariot racing contests—provided that their fathers or husbands had transferred ownership of the horses to them.

Fig. 8. Chariot race with teams of four horses. Scene on a drinking cup from around 540 B.C.

Three teams of horses race along the track at breakneck speed. The charioteers, wrapped in long garments, use crops to urge the horses on. The spectators expected daredevil passing maneuvers. The charioteer in the lead makes the mistake of turning around to look for his pursuers. Experience tells us that failing to constantly watch one's own horses almost invariably led to disaster. Even though the charioteers risked life and limb during races, it was not they but the owners of the horses who won the glory of victory.

Cyniska, the daughter of a Spartan king, won a victory each during the Olympic Games of 396 and 392 B.C. During the first century A.D. a certain Cassia from Elis won the four-foal race.

Chariot races took place in the Hippodrome. They were held in different categories. On the one hand, the Greeks distinguished between two-horse races (*synorís*) and four-horse races (*téthrippon*). The more popular four-horse races went over a distance of seventy-two stades (15,118 yards), and the two-horse chariots had to race forty-eight stades (10,079 yards). A further distinction was that between grown horses and foals. Finally, there were also races with mules and mares, but only for a limited time period—they were part of the Olympic program only at some Games during the fifth century. Emperor Nero's much-quoted ten-horse chariot is evidently part of the malicious insinuations by his political enemies, the many conservative Romans who were suspicious of him on account of his strong Grecophile tendencies (see chapter 17). During the race, the charioteer stood in the cart, holding the reins as well as a stick (*kéntron*) in his hands (fig. 8). His standard attire was a long, sleeveless garment (*chitón*) that reached down to his feet and was tied around his chest lest it flare during the breakneck race and turn into a dangerous obstacle. The horses were yoked to the harness at the tip of the hitch. The two outer horses of the four-horse chariot were directly connected to the cart by way of leather straps.

It was of paramount importance to get to the top of the field on the long straight stretches of the racecourse, which usually required difficult maneuvers to pass the other contestants. Victory, however, largely depended on how skillfully the charioteer negotiated the tight turns at the turning marks (*nyssa*). He obviously had to slow down so as not to be thrown out of the track. Yet if he decelerated too much, he lost his advantage. Both passing others and driving around the turning points was extremely dangerous. This provided the kind of drama that made the races so especially attractive to the spectators.

The equestrian contests also took place in the Hippodrome.

Without saddle and stirrup, riding was utterly exhausting and, therefore, done only over short distances.

THE HERALDS AND TRUMPETERS

It was inconceivable that the cult festival with its athletic events and their tens of thousands of spectators could have run smoothly without announcements and signals, which had to be made loudly and with fitting ceremoniousness. This task was performed by heralds and trumpeters. From the early fourth century B.C. on, heralds and trumpeters were given the opportunity to measure their skills in an actual competition whose winner also received a victor's wreath. Musical competitions, however, such as were held in Delphi, for instance, were never part of the Olympic program.

SEPARATION BY AGE GROUPS

The athletes who entered the Olympic contests were divided into two age groups. Grown men (*andres*) competed against one another in one group. The boys (*paides*) contended separately from them for the victor's crown. The groups were not strictly separated according to chronological age. Rather, the intent behind the separation was to form groups of athletes according to ability. One of the most important tasks of the judges (*agonothétei*) was to preassess the athletes' ability and assign them to their appropriate groups before the actual contests. Race horses were similarly assessed. Here the judges had to decide whether an animal was still a foal or had to be regarded as a grown horse.

The judges' assessment clearly had a tremendous impact on an athlete's chances of winning a contest. Since their verdict was heavily based on subjective criteria, the entire procedure was always clouded by suspicions of corruption. Therefore, it is not surprising that the much-quoted Olympic oath included the judges as well. Pausanias, in his description mentioned repeatedly, informs us in detail about the oath:

(The Zeus statue in the Bouleuterion) is of all the images of Zeus the one most likely to strike terror into the hearts of sinners. He is surnamed Oath-god, and in each hand he holds a thunderbolt. Beside this image it is the custom for athletes, their fathers and their brothers, as well as their trainers, to swear an oath upon the slices of boar's flesh that in nothing will they sin against the Olympic games. The athletes take this further oath also, that for ten successive months they have strictly followed the regulations for training. An oath is also taken by those who examine the boys, or the foals entering for races, that they will decide fairly and without taking bribes. . . .

(Pausanias V 24, 9–10[4])

THE PRIZES OF VICTORY

Once the contests were completed and the winners had been declared, there began a sequence of presentation ceremonies, most of which, however, did not take place at the sanctuary itself.

The ritual of the presentation ceremony at the sanctuary was confined to two acts. First came the crowning of the winner. The branches of the wreath were cut from those trees that were considered holy in the pertinent sanctuary. At Olympia, this was the olive tree, in Delphi, the laurel tree, in Isthmia, the pine tree, and in Nemea, ivy. After they were crowned with their wreaths, the victors received an additional distinction: they had a festive meal with the dignitaries of the sanctuary.

An Olympic victory generally entailed the privilege of dedicating a statue in the sanctuary that was meant to commemorate the victory, but was, of course, also a thank offering to Zeus. The specifications of the statue and the place where it was to be put had to be arranged with the sanctuary administration.

Once an Olympic champion returned to his hometown, additional honors were bestowed on him. One of them was that a purple ribbon was attached to him that henceforth distin-

4. *Description of Greece*, vol. 2, tr. W. H. S. Jones and H. A. Ormerod, Loeb Classical Library 188 (Cambridge, Mass.: Harvard University Press, 1977; first printed in 1927), p. 529.

guished him as a victorious athlete. What was more important
than all the symbolic distinctions was that he could now also
make a hefty profit from his success. Cities often offered valuable rewards as an incentive to their local athletes. In Athens,
in the sixth century B.C., the prize for a victory at Olympia was
five hundred drachmas, which was significantly more than the
median annual income. To this were added life-long exemption
from taxes and free food. Finally, a victor had a good chance of
receiving an important post in his city. The Olympic champions,
who were famous throughout the Mediterranean, were often
given diplomatic posts.

While Olympia, Delphi, Nemea, and Isthmia did not actually
pay their champions money, all other sanctuaries tried to
attract the athletes by offering considerable material rewards.
In Athens, the victors received oil from the Athena sanctuary's
rich supplies. What is more, Athens also gave the successful
athletes a sales permit. For instance, the victor of a chariot race
in Athens could make of profit of up to seven thousand drachmas from the sale of the oil he received, which was far more
than ten annual salaries! Eleusis with its famous Demeter
shrine gave the victors large amounts of grain, and in
Marathon, they received silverware. Pellene, a place in Arcadia
where animals were abounding, tried to entice athletes with
garments made of locally produced wool.

We only want to hint at the fact that quite a number of athletes failed morally on account of all these material entice-
ments: for a long time fraud, bribery, and downright buying
one's victory were part of the struggle for glory at athletic contests. It is clearly noticeable, however, that news about such
offenses decreased drastically during the era of the Roman
Empire. There are many indications for the positive impact of
the athletes' guilds' strict statutes. That the old weakness of
corruptibility was overcome was probably one of the reasons
why the institution of the Olympic Games lasted for so long.

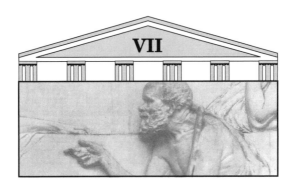

PHILOSOPHERS AGAINST ATHLETES

"Greece has many ills, but the worst one is the class of athletes!" This angry statement was put into the mouth of an actor by the playwright Euripides in his play *Autolycus* in the late fifth century B.C. Euripides jeers at athletes as "servants of their masticatory organs" and "slaves of their stomachs"—an allusion to the athletes' muscle-building diet. Yet it was not the athletes alone who were the dramatist's targets. He also harshly judged the masses who fell for these charlatans: the citizens of Greece's cities, he said, had better see to it that they were ruled by wise statesmen than regularly thronging into Olympia only to cheer at some individuals for whom gluttony was their elixir of life. He is particularly critical of the politicians for letting all this happen out of sheer populism, which made them responsible for the disintegration of true virtues. Thus Euripides' dressing-down, formulated in the fifth century B.C., culminated in his call for doing away with the Olympic contests!

Diogenes, too, who lived in the fourth century B.C., reflected on the goings-on at Olympia's venues. A representative of Cynic philosophy, he made an extremely trenchant suggestion regarding the remodeling of Olympia. Diogenes started out with a pun: the Greek word for athletes was the noun *athlaetae—*

which clearly connected it with the adjective *athlius*, which meant something like "miserable, pitiful, wretched, for the dogs." Linguistic logic, Diogenes' provocative conclusion was, cogently suggested that animals were meant to compete at Olympia.

Four hundred years later, the architecture historian Vitruvius gave vent to his frustration in his private study. He was tortured by the distinct possibility of the new book he was working on once again finding no readers. That, he claimed, was the scholar's inevitable lot. Even though scholarly books were a genuine help in dealing with life, hardly anyone ever took notice of them. While one should really expect those in responsible political positions to be keen on having these wise ideas bandied about, all that those in charge were ever interested in was favoring some athletes who happened to be successful at the moment. Indignant about this discrimination against philosophers, Vitruvius asked what good it did humanity if an athlete had at some point been undefeated in an Olympic contest.

Even this small selection of critical voices leaves no doubt that *at no time in history* was the class of Greek athletes unquestioned. The earliest documents of this kind date from the seventh century B.C. Quite clearly, however, the circle of critics confined itself to intellectuals. While their individual focus varied, they all directed their criticism at the fact that athletes were one-sided because they were too strictly fixated on very narrow physical abilities. Their necessarily egocentric way of life, the argument went, was detrimental to the common good.

The pragmatists among the critics pointed out that successful athletes were hardly ever at home and instead, competing at one of the numerous contests somewhere in Greece. Yet even when they happened to be in their hometown, they were unproductive, for their special diet and training strengthened only certain muscles, thus making their bodies useless for the crucial tasks of military service and the procurement of food (Tyrtaeus, seventh century B.C.; Xenophanes, sixth century B.C.).

The circle around Plato recognized the danger of inhibiting one's intellectual development by strictly focusing on the functioning of one's muscles. Only those who did exercises or gymnastics in order to stay healthy, and who furthermore advanced their musical education, would be able to master life's true challenges (Socrates). According to another line of reasoning, agriculture was good for exercising the body, especially since it also gave the skin a noble-looking tan (Xenophon).

The ancients' debate on high-performance sports often noticeably contains a certain element of class conceit. Let the athletes win their victories at Olympia—true success was reserved for those fit for higher education and proving their championship in equestrian sports and hunting (Isocrates, turn of the fifth to the fourth centuries B.C.).

One of the reasons for the ambivalence of ancient texts about the value of physical training was a debate among specialists that had started in the fourth century and concerned the right kind of athletic training: was it better to build strength and teach movement and technique, or was it preferable to familiarize the athletic novice with the natural motions of his body?

What did the spectators think of these debates? There is nothing that indicates that the successful athletes were ever regarded critically. The athletic contests—particularly those at Olympia—were always so popular that many a politician considered success in sports a stepping stone to his career. The young Athenian politician Alcibiades, for instance, may have crossed the line of what seems acceptable. During the so-called Peloponnesian War, that major conflict between Athens and Sparta mentioned above (chapter 3), Alcibiades sought to obtain the military command of an expedition to Sicily. To beat his rivals, he decided to enhance his reputation by becoming an Olympic champion. In order to achieve that, he didn't even have to compete personally, for even someone lacking the necessary athletic skills had a chance of capturing a winner's wreath as long as his horses came in first at a race won by an experienced charioteer for him. By sending no less than seven chariots into the race, Alcibiades did indeed return from the games an Olympic victor (Thucydides VI 15–16).

Yet this kind of misuse of the Olympic contests' popularity should not blind us to the fact that the general population held accomplished athletes in extremely high regard. During the last three centuries B.C., there were more and more instances where athletic champions were almost worshiped like gods. Popular belief attributed to them the power to heal. There was a veritable cult around some statues of champions. The example of the boxer Theagenes from the isle of Thasos illustrates this very well.

Theagenes achieved his major victories during the first decades of the fifth century B.C. He was said to have won more than 1,300 contests. In 480 and 476 B.C. he was victorious at Olympia. Consequently his native town of Thasos erected a statue on the market square in his honor. Soon it was rumored that it possessed healing power. An area around the statue was demarcated for those making it the destination of a pilgrimage. There is an inscription dated from the first century B.C. listing the sacred statutes of the Theagenes cult, which by then was in full swing. Olympia, too, had a cult around the statue of a former Olympic champion that was said to possess healing powers: that of the boxer Polydamas.

We know of at least seven such cults around the healing powers of statues of former Olympic champions. The memory of their athletic successes was magnified by tales of extraordinary achievements. These cult legends typically picked up motifs from the popular Hercules myths. In analogy to the legendary hero's accomplishments, the athletes were glorified as men who had saved lives and established order, and helped others in all imaginable kinds of distress.

Around the time of Christ the worship of athletes reached its peak. It is no coincidence that this was a historic period when many new religious movements fell on fertile ground in the Mediterranean. Yet while most of these religions reached Greece via the Orient (Mithras, Isis, Christendom), religious veneration of athletes was rooted in Greece itself.

If we encounter mainly rejection and criticism of athletes in ancient sources, we have to take this as the opinion of an intellectual minority that, however, was not able to cloud the general public's favorable view of athletic champions and events. In any case, as the main location for athletic contests, Olympia's and its cult festival's reputation and popularity grew still more. In the sixth century B.C. at the latest, Olympia became synonymous with athletic competitions in Greece. For a brief period of time its incomparable reputation made Olympia even the capital of an almost united Greece.

THE BIRTH OF THE
OLYMPIC IDEA

At the beginning of the fifth century B.C., the Persians tried twice to subjugate the cities in the Greek motherland, just as they had successfully done during the preceding decades with the Greek settlements on the west coast of Asia Minor. Considering how much the Greek districts were at variance with each other, a Persian invasion certainly promised to repeat their earlier success. In 490 B.C. Greece—in particular Athens— barely avoided a disaster at the battle near Marathon. Yet by no means did this reduce the conflict among Greek cities. Oblivious to reality, they almost lost their independence.

In 480 Persia, better prepared this time, advanced once again to the Greek mainland. The Greeks were in a subdued mood. Many cities voluntarily capitulated before the seemingly invincible enemies. Even the oracle at Delphi painted the future in dark colors. At the last minute, at least some of the Greek cities joined in an emergency alliance that included Athens, Sparta, and Corinth, among others. One after the other, the initial defense lines on land and water had to be abandoned. The city of Athens with its territories had already fallen into the hands of the pillaging Persians, when the situation finally turned around in favor of the Greeks. At first the fleet near the isle of

Salamis celebrated a surprise victory that could be witnessed from Athens (480 B.C.). Then it turned out that the forces in the plane of Plataea (479 B.C.) were also superior. When the Greeks finally prevailed against the Persian fleet near Mykale by the Ionic coast (479 B.C.), the danger of Greece being incorporated into the Persian empire was finally averted.

Greece knew that it was mainly a handful of military leaders who had saved the country: Miltiades, Leonidas, and—in the war's final phase—Themistocles. The latter's fame had not yet paled when he attended the cult festival at Olympia in 476 B.C. Everyone gathered around him to cheer him all day long—to his great satisfaction, but much to the dismay of the athletes, who for once were not the center of attention (Plutarch, *Themistocles* 17).

Yet the Greeks assembled in Olympia did not confine themselves to shouting jubilantly. The memory of the danger that had been averted, with a great deal of courage and even more good luck, also caused them to reflect on their situation. If all internal conflicts had not for once been put aside in the hour of need, a disaster would have been inevitable.

This insight marked the birth of the idea of henceforth settling all arguments among Greeks without the use of force. Instead, in the future a neutral arbitration court was to have the last word. The Zeus sanctuary in Olympia was given the honorous task of appointing a pertinent committee from among its cult administrators.

The excavations at Olympia brought to light a document from this arbitration court. Engraved in a sheet of bronze were two verdicts the Olympian arbitration court had pronounced soon after it was founded between 476 and 472 B.C. The first case involved litigation between the neighbors Boeotia and Athens. The verdict of the lower court was confirmed. In the second case, the arbiters, granting an appeal submitted by the Thessalians, waived the payment of damages to the city of Thespiae to which they had been sentenced.

Through its arbitration court, which was generally recognized, Olympia became the symbol of harmony among all Greek states. For the first time the term "divine peace" (*ekecheiria*) appeared in connection with the competitions at Olympia.

History has taught us that Olympia was not able to maintain its role as a place of conciliation among Greek cities for a long time. Still, once conjured up, the Olympic idea of peace had an impact on the next generation, independent of how quickly it actually failed. In the course of the fifth and fourth centuries B.C. many admonishers came to Olympia to appeal urgently to the Greeks once again to reconcile (Herodotus, Gorgias, Lysias, Isocrates). And it is certainly no coincidence that it was at Olympia that Alexander the Great had a proclamation read concerning an end to the plight of the refugees in the wake of the civil wars.

Even though the Eleian dream of assuming a dominating position in the world of Greek states in the years after the Persian Wars was only short-lived, the cult festival of 476 B.C. with all its hopes and promises was to remain a highlight in the history of the sanctuary, never to be forgotten.

In the chronicle of the sanctuary written around 400 B.C. by the local historian Hippias (see chapter 1) the year 476 is not particularly highlighted. Still, it probably did play a key part in Hippias' work. Lacking all pertinent facts, Hippias—as already mentioned—was forced to fill in the gaps with inventions, especially when it came to Olympia's early years. This concerned most notably the dating of the first Olympic Games. Hippias leads us back to the year 776 B.C. To us, who chose the birth of Christ as the fixed point of our chronology and since then have used the decimal system for indicating longer periods of time, the date 776 seems innocuous, because it is not a "round number" and therefore so inconspicuous.

And yet, the date 776 B.C. conceals a game with a round number: if one starts out with the key date 476 B.C. and assumes that it was preceded by a period consisting of the round number of seventy-five Olympics, one reaches the year 776 B.C. (75 x 4 = 300; 476 + 300 = 776). When in the waning fifth century

Hippias was confronted with the task of placing Olympia's early history within a chronological entity, he apparently let himself be inspired by the glorious caesura of the "jubilation Olympics" after the Persian Wars. He even turned the idea of peace, originating in 476 B.C., into a part of that early history, as the—fictitious—treaty between Iphitus and Lycurgus, which he placed in 776 B.C., already contained an agreement on a truce during the Olympic competitions.

The only historic truth in all this is the caesura of the year 476 B.C. It also left traces in Olympia's external appearance that we cannot possibly overlook.

TEMPLE AND ALTAR

The choice, in 476 B.C., of Olympia as the seat of the arbitration court for all Greeks further enhanced its reputation. The Eleians decided to use this opportunity to bestow still greater glory on the site and its festival. The peak of their newly gained self-confidence was the decision to honor Zeus by erecting a temple in his honor.

The size of the building the Eleians dedicated to him surpassed all other temples on the Peloponnesus. It rose more than 65 feet above a plot of approximately 92 by 210 feet. Its architectural structure followed the pattern typical of the Greek motherland in the fifth century B.C.: a portico surrounded on all four sides a core building that in turn consisted of three parts. The main room, the so-called *cella*, was accessible from an vestibule in the east, the so-called *pronaos*. It contained particularly precious oblations. Above all, the Cella housed the large sculpture of the seated Zeus (see fig. 10), which we will discuss shortly. The presentation ceremony with the crowning of the victorious athletes took place in the vestibule. Another room, the so-called *opisthodom*, was on the west side of the main room, in the back. It was a mirror image of the vestibule, but without access to the Cella. Measuring 16.4 x 42.5 feet, this adjoining room was large enough to also serve as a lecture hall.

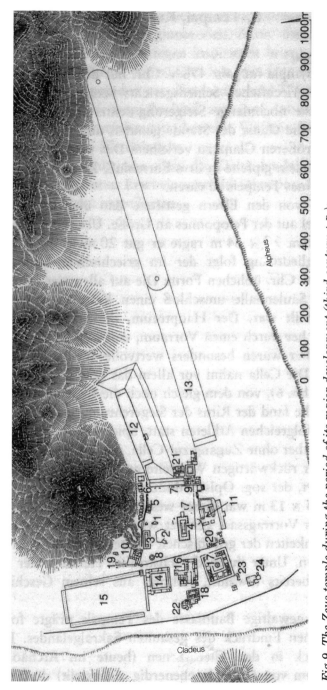

Fig 9. The Zeus temple during the period of its major development (third century A.D.):
(1) Altar of Zeus; (2) monument of Pelops; (3) temple (so-called *haion*), dedicated to Zeus or Hera around 600 B.C. by the people of Triphylia; (4) temple dedicated to Zeus around 470 by the Eleians; (5) temple dedicated to Demeter ca. 400 B.C.; (6) artificially built terrace for oblations (so-called treasury house terrace); (7) training yard with Echo Hall in front; (8) Philippeion; (9) Prytaneion from the fifth century B.C.; (10) Prytaneion after it was relocated during the period of the Roman emperors; (11) Bouleuterion; (12) Stadium (after being remodeled in the fifth century B.C.; (13) Hippodrome; (14) and (15) Gymnasion with rooms for intellectual instruction (14) and physical education (15); (16) sanctuary administration (?); (17) and (18) guest houses; (19) dining pavilion with bath; (20) shops and bath; (21) buildings for miscellaneous purposes with assembly hall, dining rooms, and baths; (22) and (23) baths; (24) clubhouse of athletes' guilds.

Famous men from the history of Greek thought appeared there, including the historian Herodotus, who, as mentioned above, read there for the first time from his historical work.

From then on the huge temple predominated the view of the entire sacred area. What attracted the visitors' gaze the most was in all probability the artwork in the pediments (which today are exhibited at ground level in Olympia's Archeological Museum). Like on a stage, both pediment areas contained decorative marble sculptures illustrating a scene from Olympia's history. Everyone who visited the temple saw its western back side from far away. Upon entering the sanctuary after traversing the Cladeus, one could make out the sculptures in the western pediment. They illustrated the myth of the interrupted wedding of the Thessalian Prince Peirithous. Aside from the members of his own tribe, the Lapiths, a guest from foreign lands, Theseus, was also invited. He had, however, tried to keep his blood relatives, the half-animal-like Centaurs (mixed creatures with a horse's body and a human torso), who lived close by, from coming by sending them deliberately late invitations. When they appeared nonetheless and after heavily imbibing began to attack the assembled guests, a wild brawl ensued. This myth clearly symbolized Greece's internal conflict. Yet Apollo, the founder and mentor of the Olympian oracle (see chapter 3), interfered and restored harmony among the adversaries. Quite obviously, in this image Olympia represented itself in its new role as the peace-making arbitration court of all Greeks.

The decorative images in the pediment on the entrance side picked up a topic that emphasized perhaps even more Olympia's significance within the world of Greek states. They served to glorify the mythic King Pelops, who gave the entire southern Greek peninsula its name. While the images illustrated the takeover of power in the Alpheus Valley, all visitors knew that this expressed Olympia's claim to control over the entire territory named after Pelops.

A variation of the concept of Olympia as the taproot and thus also the political center of the Peloponnesus, which the eastern pediment illustrates, is found in the images inside the temple. Altogether twelve square relief plates (*metopes*) on the smaller sides of the center building, the Cella, celebrate the deeds of Hercules. Hercules was the "national hero" of those Greeks who considered themselves members of the Doric tribe. Yet the Dorians' central territory—though not their native land—was the Peloponnesus.

To us, this overtly political component seems inappropriate for a temple, which we regard as the sanctuary's central place of worship. While this view expresses a concept that is familiar to us, it misses the essence of the practice of religion in ancient Greece. Certain exceptions aside, a cult was practiced not at the temple, but at the altar under the open sky. Some sanctuaries never even had a temple. Upon closer examination, at sites where a temple seems to constitute the center of the sanctuary, it almost always turns out to have been built at a relatively late stage of the sanctuary's development. This is true for Olympia as well.

If a temple was not an edifice central to a cult, why do we still find so many similar-looking temples in Greek sanctuaries? What convention do they hide?

We are still largely in the dark about the origins of Greek temple construction. One reason for erecting a building at a place of worship could be hidden in a custom of Greece's early aristocratic society: the men who made the decisions in their community typically gathered at the fireside. The sacred character of the assembly place bestowed the council's decisions with more authority. Such assembly houses with a central fireside (so-called "fireside temples") were discovered in several sanctuaries.

The assembly buildings at the Holy Fireside were visible signs of a community unity. Transformed into stone and developed into an art form, temples contain this symbolic meaning. This also explains the phenomenon of the temples always being donations by the cities in charge of the sanctuaries.

With the clear message contained in the images of the

Olympian Zeus temple, it constitutes an excellent example of a temple that was erected by its local community—in this case, the Eleians—in an act of proud self-representation. The Eleians themselves referred to the building as an offering to Zeus as thanks for his aid in conquering the Alpheus Valley and thus in taking over the Zeus sanctuary. They also bandied about the information that the huge edifice was financed through war booty.

This fact makes us look at the second temple in Olympia, which was built some 130 years before the Temple of Zeus, around 600 B.C., at the foot of the Gaion (fig. 9, no. 3). This temple is said to have been dedicated by the city of Scillus (Pausanias V 16, 1). Scillus was located in Triphylia; in other words, its inhabitants were the ones originally in charge of Olympia. The people of Scillus had defended themselves vehemently against the Eleians' conquest of the Alpheus Valley. Consequently, the Eleians hated the city so much they destroyed it (Pausanias V 6, 4).

Yet when the Eleians conquered Olympia, they were not allowed to destroy the citizens of Scillus's old oblation. That would have been a serious sacrilege. The Eleians did away with their enemies' temple in a more subtle way, by erecting the enormous, magnificent temple that made the Triphylian city's modest edifice almost disappear in comparison. The Eleians probably even went a step further by transferring the Triphylians' temple to a different god. We know the building as Temple of Hera. More recent research, however, has determined that at the time it was consecrated by the citizens of Scillus, it was probably dedicated to the lord of the sanctuary, Zeus.

Antiquity has given us no clue about what triggered the erection of the third temple in Olympia (fig. 9, no. 5). It was dedicated to (De-)Meter, who was worshiped even back in Olympia's early days. She was often the focus of attention during the sanctuary's long history (see also chapter 16).

If the temples in the Zeus sanctuary did not serve as sites where the local cult was exercised, the images of the gods inside

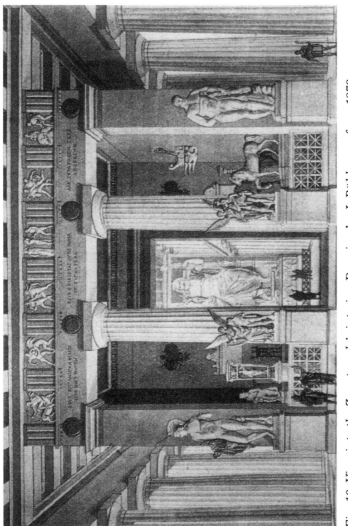

Fig. 10. View into the Zeus temple's interior. Drawing by J. Bühlmann from 1873.

Only a few Greek temples had a specific function in the practice of a cult. They were usually oblations in which other artifacts dedicated to the god were stored. Bühlmann's imaginative drawing gives us an idea of what the Zeus Temple must have looked like. In the back we recognize an oversize statue: the almost forty-foot-high statue of the seated Zeus with its surface made of gold and ivory. Phidias' masterwork was one of the Seven Wonders of the World, constituting one of Olympia's main attractions.

can hardly have been cult images. This is also true for the Eleians' almost forty-foot-high statue of the seated Zeus in his temple (fig. 10). The surface of the statue was skillfully assembled from gold and ivory. The Eleians had been able to commission the great sculptor Phidias for this work, which became instantly famous. Like the Temple of Zeus, so the Zeus statue inside it was financed through booty from the war against the Triphylians, and was meant to immortalize the Eleians' thanks for their victory.

Phidias' Zeus, in other words, was not a cult image but a particularly precious thank-offering from the Eleians to their god.

Cult images proper—that is to say, statues that were directly involved in cult activities—seem to have been very rare. In any event, they are rarely mentioned in Greek sanctuaries. To cite some examples: as part of the cult festival, the image of Hera on the isle of Samos was carried to the nearby coast, cleaned off, and decorated. During her festival on the fortress mountain of Athens, Athena received a new garment. In the Aphaea sanctuary on Aegina and the Hera sanctuary by Foce del Sele near Paestum, the cult legend about the goddess' landing in a boat was represented as a scene in which the goddess' statue was used. In these cases we can call the temples' statues of the goddesses actual cult images. This does not, however, apply to the famous Athena Parthenus in the Parthenon on the Acropolis in Athens, but it does to the simple statue of the seated Athena in her old temple, which was later replaced by the Erechtheion in the fifth century B.C.

With the exception of very few sites, the sacred center of every sanctuary was always the altar. The Zeus Altar in Olympia (fig. 2, no. 4; fig. 9, no. 1) belongs to the group of ash altars. The term is derived from the ashes accumulating at the sacrificial fire, which were not removed but skillfully formed into an ever larger cone (fig. 3). The altar also served as the site of the oracle (see chapter 3). Therefore, the seers were responsible for tending to the altar. Even when the Zeus sanctuary had lost its role as oracle site during the era of Roman emperors, the seers remained in office, as they continued to be in charge of the ash altar of Zeus.

Today there is no longer any trace of the ash altar. The text by Pausanias, however, which we have quoted several times (V 13, 8–11), contains a detailed description of its form, its maintenance, and some of the rites performed there:

> The altar of Olympic Zeus. . . has been made from the ash of the thighs of the victims sacrificed to Zeus. . . . The first stage of the altar at Olympia, called *prothysis*, has a circumference of one hundred and twenty-five feet; the circumference of the stage on the *prothysis* is thirty-two feet; the total height of the altar reaches to twenty-two feet. The victims themselves it is the custom to sacrifice on the lower stage, the *prothysis*. But the thighs they carry up to the highest part of the altar and burn them there. The steps that lead up to the *prothysis* from either side are made of stone, but those leading from the *prothysis* to the upper part of the altar are, like the altar itself, composed of ashes. The ascent to the *prothysis* may be made by maidens, and likewise by women, when they are not shut out from Olympia, but men only can ascend from the *prothysis* to the highest part of the altar. Even when the festival is not being held, sacrifice is offered to Zeus by private individuals and daily by the Eleians. Every year the soothsayers, keeping carefully to the nineteenth day of the month Elaphius, bring the ash from the town-hall, and make it into a paste with the water of the Alpheius they daub the altar therewith.[1]

If, therefore, the temples and the statues of the gods inside were part of the group of oblations expressing a sanctuary's self-assessment and claim, then the altar was the site where the cult was practiced. For this reason, the size and design of the altar site is invariably an indication of how many pilgrims visited the sanctuary.

---

1. *Description of Greece*, tr. W. H. S. Jones and H. A. Ormerod, vol. 2, Loeb Classical Library 188 (Cambridge, Mass.: Harvard University Press, 1977; first printed in 1927), pp. 455–57.

THE THEATER

From the seventh century B.C. on, athletic competitions were at the center of Olympia's cult festival. The Zeus sanctuary did not offer artistic performances of the same standard as Apollo's festival at Delphi, for instance. Therefore, it does not come as a surprise that the excavated ruins of Olympia did not reveal the semicircle, characteristically made of stone, of a Greek theater.

Still, Olympia's Zeus sanctuary did have a theater. This is mentioned almost in passing in an ancient report on the site (Xenophon, *Hellenika* VII 4, 31). Since the spectator stands of Greek theaters were usually built on natural slopes, archeologists searched the Cronus foothills for possible traces of that theater, but to no avail.

Only when the topographic directions in the ancient texts were taken seriously did it become absolutely clear where to look for the theater (*theatron*): it must have been northeast of the Zeus Temple and north of the Hestia sanctuary in the *prytaneion* of the classical period (fig. 9, no. 9). Thus there can be no doubt that the Olympian theater was the altar site, with its grandstand-like boundaries in the east and the north (fig. 11).

In the northern part of the altar site the audience could use the terraced foot of the Cronus Hill as an ideal place from which to witness what was happening at the altar site. The terrace's

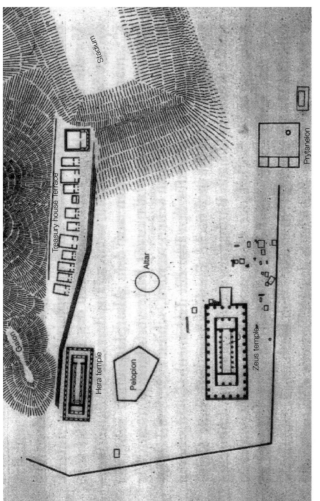

Fig. 11. Olympia's theater.

The highlight of the cult festival was the offering of the sacrifice at the Altar of Zeus. The procession's entry into the center of the sanctuary was already a magnificent spectacle no festival attendant would want to miss. When the sanctuary and festival were again upgraded after 476 B.C., a large area was raised for the spectator stands east of the altar site. Along with the treasury house terrace, it formed the Theatron documented in ancient sources. In the fourth century B.C. there were plans to replace the eastern embankment with covered stands ("Echo Hall"). But construction was halted and the audience had to be content with an alternative solution (wooden stands?) until the late first century B.C.

thirteen-foot-high retaining wall, ascending in steps, offered additional room for the spectators. Significantly more room was created during the major reconstruction of the sanctuary in the 470s B.C., when, at the same time the Zeus Temple was built, the tall earthwork between the altar site and the Stadium was raised to form a double spectator stand. The hillside sloping to the west formed a part of the *theatron*, and the one on the eastern embankment accommodated spectators of the competitions in the Stadium.

One hundred years after the major extension of the Theatron illustrated in fig. 11, the theater was reconstructed more substantially. Half of the eastern embankment was leveled. Only the slope toward the Stadium remained. In the area thus gained was built a court approximately 110 yards long and 9 yards wide. Half of it was covered by a roof. Here, directly by the venues, the athletes at last had room for their final preparations for the performances in the Stadium and the Hippodrome (see chapter 11).

The plan was to take advantage of the removal of the original stands to reconstruct them in the contemporary style. In front of the 110-yard-long west wall of the training ground was to be put a vestibule from which the events at the altar site could have been followed much better than previously. As we shall see (chapter 15), it even seems that there was a sponsor offering to build a spectator hall at the sanctuary. Political developments, however, dried up this source soon after construction began. At least the elevated socle of the hall was finished. On it were erected wooden stands during the festivals so that the Theatron continued to be in use.

What did the spectators at the sanctuary see when they took their seats in the Theatron, from where they had approximately the view illustrated in fig. 3?

There can be no doubt that the athletic competitions were the main attraction of the cult festival in Olympia. Yet what has been written very clearly about so many other cult festivals in Greek cities is true for Olympia as well: the greatest moment for any active or passive participant of any cult festival was the arrival of the procession at the festival site. Everyone of rank had a part in this. All citizens' groups were represented. Obviously, the local population was particularly keen on identifying the numerous festival legations from other cities, as their number and origin was a reflection on the reputation of the city organizing the festival.

After the reconstruction of the Theatron, the cult festival's program was extended: from the 472 B.C. Olympics on, an entire day—the third of the five-day celebration—was reserved for sacrificial offerings at the altar. Once again the spectators gathered on the theater stands in order to observe the festive activities. And finally, the theater seats were sought after at the end of the competitions, when the victors were crowned in the vestibule of the Zeus Temple. After all, the temple's front side was basically a part of the Theatron's setting (see fig. 3) and, therefore, a perfect site for the presentation ceremony.

Once, during the 104th Olympics in 364 B.C., the spectators took their seats in the Theatron to watch the wrestling matches, which were being held as the last part of the pentathlon, from high up above. This was probably the only time the Theatron was used for athletic competitions. That year, however, was an exception: it was the cult festival which, much to the Eleians' chagrin, was organized by the Arcadians after they had reappropriated the Alpheus Valley and the sanctuary (see chapter 1).

A theater such as the Zeus sanctuary's in Olympia was by no means unique. Anyone roaming through Greek sanctuaries with eyes wide open will notice that time and time again, halls or steps line the surroundings of the altar sites. There are even several indications that, in the final analysis, Greek temples were surrounded by columns to give the temple walls some shade. This way the activities in the center of the sacred place could be observed under more comfortable conditions than would have been possible without the protection of the colonnades.

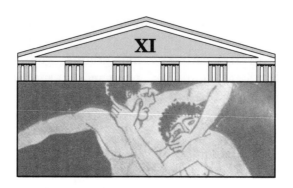

PREPARATION AND TRAINING

By the time the competitions began, the athletes had gone through a long preparation phase in Olympia. Ever since the Zeus sanctuary was administrated by Elis (see chapter 1), the contenders had to gather there before the cult festival started. Watching the athletes train, the chief judges (*hellanodikae*) divided them into groups so that athletes of similar qualification would encounter each other in the preliminary rounds. In cases of doubt about which age group an athlete belonged to, this was also the time when the decision was made whether young athletes would compete with boys or with men (see chapter 14). Since the athletes lived together in Elis, their nutrition could be monitored, so no secret recipes for specific muscle-building food (doping) could be administered. These preparations took place at the local gymnasiums (Pausanias VI 23).

The athletes did not enter the Zeus sanctuary until the Eleians' procession arrived at the festival site in the Alpheus Valley. We are familiar with the particulars of how they were accommodated and how they trained in Olympia only for the competitions from the third century B.C. on. In the western section of the sacred area a *gymnasion* had been erected (fig. 9, nos. 14 and 15). As we shall see later (see chapter 14), the *gym-*

nasion at the Zeus sanctuary in Olympia was certainly not built exclusively for the athletic contenders. During the festival, however, that is where they were based. The athletes' quarters were in the west wing of the complex for track-and-field practice (fig. 9, no. 15), directly next to the quay by the Cladeus. The contestants could, of course, continue their training in the large building complex. Before the third century B.C.—when the original *gymnasion* and the accommodations were replaced by stone constructions—the athletes stayed in tents, just like the festival attendants (see chapter 13).

For the athletes, accommodations where they could warm up before the competition were just as important as uninterrupted training. Depending on the type of sport they competed in, they needed a place to store their equipment. Finally, since competitions were in the nude, they needed a place to keep their clothes. The charioteers, on the other hand, had to put on a special outfit that was laced up in an intricate manner. After the competition, they naturally had to clean up. For that purpose, the athletes applied a thick layer of oil to their sweaty, dust-covered skin, and removed the entire coat of dirt from their bodies with a bronze scraper (*strigilis*). The rooms for these procedures had to be reasonably close to the Stadium and the Hippodrome.

Since the mid-fourth century B.C. the athletes had a room that was ideally situated: the court, approximately nine yards wide and over one hundred yards long, directly behind the so-called Echo Hall (fig. 9, no. 7). Half of that court was covered by a roof. The two narrow sides had doors that could be locked. The northern side led directly to the tunnel-like Stadium access way, and in the south one could quickly get to the Hippodrome's starting blocks. Recent excavations in the Zeus sanctuary in Nemea unearthed a building with the exact same function, and similarly situated.

As we saw earlier, the Zeus sanctuary in Olympia was not constructed as a site for athletic competitions. Therefore, it does not come as a surprise if we cannot establish the first real stadium at Olympia until 700 B.C. (fig. 2, no. 11), almost four hun-

Fig 12. The Stadium as it was built around 470 B.C. (reconstruction after its excavation).
The track is 209.73 yards long and approximately 34 yards wide. Twenty runners could compete simultaneously. The earth embankment, for the most part built artificially, accommodated some 40,000 spectators. The Hippodrome (which still has not been excavated) was parallel to the (in the illustration, left) long side in the south.

dred years after the cult originated.

One consideration for choosing the area in the eastern part of the sanctuary must have been that the plateaus there could be used as a natural grandstand area along the north side of the running tracks. On the narrow side in the east and in the south, however, the ground had to be raised. The resulting wall could serve as a double stand, as the area bordering on its south side was part of the Hippodrome.

Originally no stands were built in the west, toward the center of the sanctuary. If one looked at the venue for the competitions and the altar site simultaneously, they were both next to each other, on the same level. This was changed drastically during the massive reconstruction decided on in 476 B.C. Between these two areas now rose the double stands for the Stadium and the Theatron mentioned in chapter 9.

Due to the wide grandstand wall in the west—its width at the bottom was 76.5 yards—the tracks had to be shifted east by that distance. They were once again made wider on that occasion, so that twenty runners could now compete at once. The walls, which were raised all around, accommodated approximately 40,000 spectators (fig. 12). The access tunnel at the Stadium's northwest corner was not constructed until three and a half centuries after the west wall was built. During that long period of time, to descend into the Stadium from the altar site, one first had to pass the treasure house terrace.

Most other famous stadiums in Greece were reconstructed once more during the reign of the Roman emperors, if not earlier. Typically the simple earthworks were furnished with stone and, on occasion, even marble seats for the spectators (e.g., Delphi, Athens, Epidaurus, and Messene). In Olympia of all places, indubitably the main venue for athletic competitions in the entire Mediterranean, no reconstruction in the new style took place. This fact is all the more remarkable as the man who arranged for and financed the stadiums in Delphi and Athens, the billionaire sponsor Herodes Atticus, was active in Olympia too and therefore probably would have been willing to become involved in reconstructing the Stadium as well (see chapter 16).

The modernization of Olympia's Stadium that did not take place is not the only enigma surrounding it. What is even more peculiar is the clause in the sanctuary's sacred law denying married women the right to watch the competitions in the Stadium, while unmarried girls were allowed to attend (Pausanias VI 20, 9). It is all the more surprising that on the other hand, in the middle of the earthwork stand, a place of honor made of stone was reserved for a woman who could certainly be married: Demeter's priestess (fig. 13).

Demeter's place of honor probably contains the key to an understanding of the peculiarities of the Olympic stadium. The cult's name for the goddess whose priestess had a place of honor in the Stadium was Chamyne, meaning "the one whose bed is on the ground." Demeter had always been part of the group of vegetation goddesses that were worshiped in the Alpheus Valley. The leveling of the ground southeast of the Cronus Hill as preparation for building the sports facilities around 700 B.C. (fig. 2, nos. 11 and 12) probably destroyed Demeter Chamyne's place of worship. The priestess' place of honor then might have been built in the Stadium, as a reminder of who the original lady of the land was. The fact that the Stadium was not expanded by way of additional stone structures can also be explained by the cult surrounding "Demeter, who rests on the ground." In that case the priestess' special status and the preservation of the ground's surface might be viewed as a sign of penance for destroying the former place of worship.

In this light it seems plausible to explain the different treatment of women in regard to granting access to the Stadium as a consequence of old sacred statutes of the Demeter/Chamyne cult. In any event, it would not be unusual if the cult of Demeter/Chamyne had been reserved for unmarried girls, who had to undergo a sequence of initiation rites as preparation for their future role as wives and mothers.

Olympia's Hippodrome was famous for the elaborate layout of its starting blocks. The horses could be directed in such a way that none of them had an advantage or disadvantage as a result of their starting position. This sophisticated system was often admired and described in antiquity. The calculations that were involved, however, were so extremely complicated that the texts very often contain mistakes and misunderstandings. Thus scholars prevailed only recently in decoding the numerical jumble in a medieval copy of a document, and in reconstructing the shape of the Hippodrome (fig. 9, no. 13). According to this text, the Hippodrome lay parallel to the Stadium, but extended for the entire length of the plane up to the hills, which enclosed it in the east (fig. 1).

Ancient descriptions of horse races indicate that spectators not only paid attention to who was leading in a race. They found the various, usually extremely risky, maneuvers at passing one another highly thrilling. The similarly dramatic maneuvers at the two turning points also attracted close attention. Between the two turning points, the Olympic Hippodrome had a length of about 650 yards and was just 65 yards wide. Spread along the entire length of the course, thousands of spectators could follow the breathtaking races from close up. This exciting atmosphere no doubt contributed greatly to the tremendous popularity of the Olympic chariot races.

After the chariot races were over, the arenas emptied. Tens of thousands of visitors set out to return to their homes. But this did not mean that the Alpheus Valley entered a four-year period of rest.

ANCIENT TOURISM BETWEEN THE FESTIVALS

The cult festival of Olympian Zeus with its numerous athletic contests was held every four years. In Old Greek, it was a "pent-eteric" festival. Literally translated, this means that it was held "every five years." This confusing way of counting requires an explanation. If we look at the time span between the cult festival of 476 B.C. and the one in 472 B.C., we have five different years: 476, 475, 474, 473, and 472. This explains why a period really covering a span of four years was called "five-year term."

After its reorganization in the fifth century B.C., the cult festival lasted five days. Once it was over, more than 1,400 days passed before the next festival began. Therefore, it may be surprising that even though the site was used so little, it was built and maintained at such an expense. Yet the notion that a sanctuary was filled with people for only a short while and then almost deserted for a long period of time is utterly wrong. Again we must keep in mind that Olympia was not specifically built as a venue.

Let us first take a look at the sequence of events during the Zeus festival itself. Naturally, such a celebration required a great deal of meticulous preparation. Visitors from far away had to be accommodated and fed. This was usually done at the sanctuary itself. The expansive festival meadow in the south of the sacred area was available for both purposes (fig. 2, no. 9). Thus the upcoming festival period was announced by the arrival of carpenters, who built the scaffoldings for tents and leaf-covered huts. The first merchants began to set up their stands, for generally markets were held as soon as the hordes of festival attendants arrived. At the end of the five festival days, disassembling all the tents and wooden constructions was a time-consuming task. Again weeks passed in which the sanctuary was filled with people and activities related to the cult festival.

Even though this is not documented, we may certainly assume that those attendants who had traveled from distant lands—for instance, from the Lower Italian colonies—extended their stay in Olympia to spend some time with their relatives and friends in the old homeland.

Many Greek cities sent official festival legations to a cult festival such as Zeus' in Olympia, all the more so if one of their citizens had reasonable hopes of winning a contest. The presence of men of influence from cities virtually all over Greece during the festival period was a welcome opportunity for political talks. This, too, could result in visitors extending their stay at Olympia. This is explicitly documented for the cult festival of 428 B.C. It was the period shortly after the Peloponnesian War, when Athens and Sparta and their respective allies were head to head with one another. Sparta's followers had agreed to meet in order to discuss current issues of warfare and the inclusion of additional allies in the Peloponnesian League, in which they were organized (Thucydides III, 14, 1).

If we consider these basic facts, which applied to all Greek cult festivals, the Olympian hurly-burly lasted quite a bit longer than the actual festival. Yet even if we assume that life in Olympia—including all preparations as well as the festival's aftermath—was solely determined by the cult festival for two or even three months, the period between two festivals was still

Fig. 13. Altar of Demeter on the wall of the Stadium's northern spectator stand.

Unlike unwed girls, married women were forbidden to enter Olympia's Stadium. Only the priestess of Demeter was exempt from this strict rule. She even received a place of honor in the Stadium next to an altar of Demeter. It is likely that the reason for the different treatment of married and unmarried women was that before the athletic installations were built, the place contained a place of worship for Demeter in which the priestess gathered unmarried girls around her before their wedding. The old cult rules were transferred to the new use of the place.

much longer than the festival itself.

Yet by no means was the period between festivals a time of rest for the sanctuary administration. After all, Greek shrines were not simply built as sites for their pertinent cult festivals. In many different ways they were a part of people's everyday life. This is of course true for Olympia as well.

We have seen that at the time it was founded, the Olympian place of worship served as a site where the inhabitants of the Alpheus Valley prayed to their vegetation gods for fertile soil. If we follow the written historical sources, the sanctuary's early visitors did not offer their oblations and prayers only to the earth goddess Gaia. Very early on, Demeter and Eileithya, the goddess of birth, were also worshiped there. Men and women came to the sanctuary with specific concerns arising from their work or their families (fig. 14). Every single day was apt to provide them with a reason to turn to their gods for help and advice, and every day the place of worship was there for them.

The oracle also filled the sanctuary with life. From what we know about other oracle sites, we may assume that Olympia was visited for extended periods by larger legations that also wanted to put questions to the oracle. Before they could call on the seers, they had to undergo certain rituals. Yet these legations didn't come merely to seek advice. Once the pertinent action was successfully completed with the oracle's assistance, the lord of the oracle, Zeus, had to be offered thanks. The legations had to negotiate with the sanctuary administration about what oblation would be appropriate and where to place it. Naturally, a new legation arrived for the ceremonious offering to the god itself.

It is obvious from these considerations alone that Olympia was always bustling with people. Yet there were many additional reasons for people to visit the sanctuary. In all likelihood, everyday life was strongly affected by the tendency to associate more and more cults with the Zeus sanctuary, which soon dominated everything around it. Specifically, old and established places of worship in the Alpheus Valley founded branches at the

Fig. 14. Clay figure of a woman giving birth, 4th–3rd century B.C.

In antiquity, women gave birth in a crouching position, as depicted in this figurine. The jar the pregnant woman takes to her mouth with her right hand may contain a tonic. The figure, which has a height of barely more than two and a half inches, is a reminder that the Zeus sanctuary was not exclusively a meeting place for male athletes. Women, too, turned to the gods with their specific concerns. As goddess of birth, *Eleithyia* had an ancient cult on the southern slope of the Hill of Cronus.

site of the Zeus sanctuary, in whose illustrious proximity they celebrated their annual cult festivals. For instance, three Artemis sanctuaries from the Alpheus Valley were transferred to Olympia (Strabo VIII 3, 12).

Over the years the number of altars within Zeus' sacred area had climbed to more than seventy. Every one of these altars attracted its own worshipers. In addition, once every month the sanctuary itself organized a procession that followed a set sequence, stopping at each of these altars to make an offering. Month after month, this all-day ritual brought a certain influx of participants and spectators.

Once a year, in the spring, a festive event took place in which a new layer was added to the ash altar of Zeus: the two priests in charge of the altar—who were identical with the seers from the families of the Iamids and Clytiads—mixed the ashes from the altar of Hestia with water from the Alpheus. They then put a coat of that mixture on the ever growing ash cone of the Altar of Zeus (fig. 3). Hestia's altar in the *prytaneion* (fig. 9, nos. 9 and 10) offered another reason for regularly visiting the sanctuary: it contained the Holy Fire that was burning for the inhabitants of Elis.

Every day an official offering was made at the altar of Zeus. Private individuals were always free to go there to turn to their god with prayers and offerings (see chapter 9).

Greek sanctuaries abounded with artifacts and magnificent buildings. Visitors were of course supposed to notice their splendor. It is not without reason that most cities had important statues from their sanctuaries' supplies stamped on their coins. A site such as Olympia, where renowned sculptors from antiquity were represented with their works, naturally attracted interested and curious crowds. The sanctuary employed staff to specifically handle this "art tourism." They are referred to as exegetes in the official lists, that is to say, as men who could explain everything. In the following chapter we will discuss the rest of the staff employed at the sanctuary.

Understandably, ancient documents about the Zeus sanctuary largely center on sports, as Olympia was synonymous with athletic contests. Still, we may assume that those who lived nearby did not look at and deal with their place of worship any differently than people did at so many other Greek sanctuaries about which we have unshakable information. Thus the sanctuaries' festival meadows were a popular site for major family celebrations. The typical sanctuary's infrastructure also lent itself to ending a happy day among family and friends with singing, dancing, and a cup of wine. In the second century B.C. the poet Nicaenetus celebrated such a get-together at a sanctuary in a poem.

How much the larger Greek sanctuaries—including Olympia —were frequented throughout the year is finally indicated by the leases of inns and hostels within the sacred area (*capeleia*; for Olympia, see fig. 9, nos. 17–21; fig. 15), from which the sanctuaries profited considerably.

Another important aspect of all Greek sanctuaries was their function as asylums. Those seeking refuge had the right to remain at the sanctuary until their matter was settled. Like the rest of the visitors staying at Olympia for an extended period, they typically camped on the festival meadow. Occasionally they made their living by doing errands and odd jobs for the sanctuary.

When the cult festival for the Olympian Zeus was approaching, the sanctuary changed its appearance noticeably. The number of people there increased day by day. No other festival captivated as many visitors. All those in responsible positions at the sanctuary would have been relieved when they had once again successfully completed the tasks the festival imposed on them. Yet not even during the periods between festivals did they have a chance to rest. Many inhabitants of the Alpheus Valley would have been relieved when the bustle of the celebrations was over and their local place of worship was once again available for them to turn to with their everyday concerns.

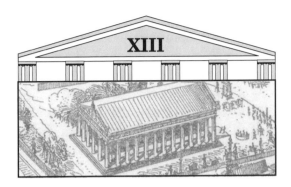

THE OLYMPIC VILLAGE

An altar and a surrounding sacred area where the cult's various rituals could be performed were the basic components of all Greek sanctuaries. The size of the sacred area depended on the character of the cult. Obviously, the design of the space was determined by the way in which the cult festival was celebrated. If the program was limited to the performance of round dances, considerably less space was needed than for festivals that included athletic contests.

The design of a sanctuary also depended on the living conditions of those who operated the place of worship and visited it regularly. Precious oblations from the upper strata of society required different designs for their presentation and storage in the sanctuary than did modest votive pictures from a less prosperous population.

This brief outline may suffice to explain why Olympia's Zeus sanctuary was among the most extravagant in Greece. Even today's ruins give us an inkling of the site's former splendor. Nonetheless, the walls that have been excavated give us but a limited impression of what the sanctuary used to look like.

Religious festivals in Greece are inconceivable without the festival attendants' social gatherings, which were welcome opportunities for eating, dancing, and merriment. The precinct with the altar and the oblations—either in the open air or in treasuries and temples—was one part of the cult site, but so was the area where the social gatherings took place. This obligatory structure of all sacred areas in Greece is particularly well documented for Olympia: in one of his Olympian Odes, Pindar described in detail how Hercules once designed the sanctuary in cooperation with Apollo:

> [He] measured out a sacred precinct for his father most
>   mighty; He fenced in the Altis and set it apart
> in the open, and he made the surrounding plain
> a resting place for banqueting . . .
>
> (Pindar, "Tenth Olympian Ode"[1])

The term for Olympia's sacred center was the Altis. It has been completely laid bare by excavations (fig. 2, nos. 1–8; see also the area in fig. 9). While we do not know the exact measurements of the "surrounding plain" mentioned in the ode, we may presume that it reached up to the Cladeus in the west (fig. 2, no. 10) and in the south was bounded by the bank of the Alpheus (fig. 2, no. 9). We have no clues as to how far it extended north, but it seems reasonable to assume that the area used by the sanctuary's visitors stretched to the upper border of figures 2 and 9. This is approximately the location of Olympia's New Museum today.

Pindar's words indicate that both areas with their entirely different functions were equally part of the sacred precinct. They are referred to here as "sacred center" and "festival meadow." Only segments of the western part of Olympia's festival meadow have been examined. Yet on the basis of these findings, we can describe the characteristics of the site's entire infrastructure.

A sanctuary as large and varied as Olympia's needed a staff to run and maintain the place appropriately. The obligatory

---

1. *Pindar I*, ed. and tr. William H. Race, Loeb Classical Library 56 (Cambridge, Mass.: Harvard University Press, 1997), p. 167.

administration buildings were located on the festival meadow, as close to the sacred center as possible (fig. 9, no. 16). This complex also contained the repair shops and studios where restorers mended damaged oblations and where artists who had specifically traveled there made statues commissioned by the sanctuary or by private donors. Among these artists was Phidias, who lived and worked in the fifth century B.C. and who was admired by subsequent generations. It was in Olympia's workshop that he created the tall statue inside the Temple of Zeus (fig. 10). In antiquity, this studio was occasionally referred to as "workshop of Phidias" in his memory.

With the exception of the administration complex, there were no actual houses on the festival meadow for centuries. This does not mean, however, that the area was undeveloped. Depending on the site's current needs, temporary buildings were constructed there. In other words, tents, leaf-covered huts, and stands were set up for the provision of room and board for visitors, or for the sale of votive artwork and commodities. These constructions could be easily disassembled during quieter periods.

A large number of Greek sanctuaries have given us clues that, when put together, give us a clear picture of this assortment of tents and huts at the edge of the sanctuary. Olympia's population started to feel the excitement of the approaching festival when the hammering began on the festival meadow that accompanied the setting up of the wooden constructions, and when the visitors from near and far began raising their often precious tarpaulins.

These constructions, put up for only short periods of time, were by no means looked at as temporary facilities. Very early on there was actual competition among the festival-goers about who was going to have the most magnificently furnished tent or hut. Statutes were discovered in some sanctuaries specifying the size of tents and admissible furnishings. The purpose of these rules was to keep visitors from going overboard in their self-display. In Olympia, for example, Alcibiades with his ostentatious tent was frowned upon (see also chapter 7). The sacred law of the sanctuary in the nearby city of Andania restricted the pilgrims' flamboyance by limiting the size of their tents and putting restrictions on their furbishings.

Lodging visitors individually on the festival meadow gave the festival officials—who from the sixth century B.C. were the Eleians—another advantage by giving them an additional means of honoring citizens and guests. We know from inscriptions in honor of people in some Greek cities that anyone of merit had the right to put up his tent at a prominent place during a cult festival.

Probably no other cult festival in Greece had such an extended tent city as the Zeus festival in Olympia with its many visitors from distant lands who all needed lodgings during their extended stay. The battle between Eleians and Arcadians during the cult festival in 364 B.C., which has been mentioned previously, gives us an idea of how many of those temporary constructions there were: to defend themselves against an Eleian attack, the Arcadians ordered all leaf-covered huts and tents to be torn down overnight. They used the planks and bars thus gained to build a protective wall around the sanctuary, and there was so much wood that the wall became high enough to discourage the Eleians from repeating their attack (Xenophon, *Hellenika* VII 4, 32).

The cult festival of Zeus took place during the hottest days in August. The proverbial dust, heat, and water shortage in Olympia's tent city were excruciating. Thus Greek masters of insubordinate slaves were often advised that the best way to reestablish discipline was not flogging or anything of that sort. Much more effective, they were told, was the terse threat of sending the slaves to Olympia, for the horror of being subjected to the conditions there would be enough to rein them in immediately (Aelian, *Varia Historia* XIV 18).

One of the many legends surrounding the early Greek natural philosopher Thales reveals a great deal about the water shortage. In antiquity the story went that Thales considered water to be nature's most precious gift, even believing it was the primary matter from which the world was created. According to a legend related by Diogenes Laertius (I 39), Thales died from thirst while staying at a gymnasium. Apparently this story was fabricated under the impression of the average conditions at the Olympian festival meadow, where the water shortage was the most extreme.

Besides the extreme crowding together between tents and huts, there were countless individual fireplaces where the visitors prepared their sumptuous meals. Consequently, greasy smoke, ashes, and added heat spread throughout the tent city.

One of the earliest attempts at creating an organized infrastructure was, therefore, the development of a water supply system. Since the Zeus sanctuary is in an area abounding in water, plenty of ground water was available. However, to make it accessible, wells had to be built. Here, too, during the first few centuries the Olympians confined themselves to making wells that were kept functioning only temporarily. Shafts were dug deep into the ground to the ground water level, and as soon as the crowds of visitors left, they were filled up again. All this work was worthwhile, not least because the often more than fifteen-foot-deep shafts were ideal for taking up all the garbage the legions of people left behind. (In this context we cannot but wonder where all these visitors relieved themselves. There were some latrines, but most of the sewage probably went into the rivers.)

These temporary wells constituted the predominant form of water supply in Olympia until the fourth century B.C. Negligence or carelessness on the part of the sanctuary administration certainly cannot explain the fact that they were used for such a long time. We may assume that there were quite pragmatic reasons for holding on to this utterly primitive way of supplying water: all Greek sanctuaries adhered to the sacred law that objects which had been offered to a god had to remain in the sanctuary, because they belonged to that god. This rule applied not only to votive objects, which had to be kept within

Fig. 15. The Leonidaeon, a meeting place for high society.

From the fourth century B.C., Olympia could offer its discriminating visitors comfortable premises for the social gatherings that were held during all cult festivals. The banquet halls were rented to festive parties as needed. Naturally, the guests' needs and how their demands were met changed over the centuries. Thus the Leonidaeon was fundamentally renovated in the late first century. The playful gardens in the center of the building complex date from that time.

the sacred precinct even if they were damaged. It also applied to everything that had been carried into the sanctuary as part of the communal meals, including dishes and the remains of the animals that had been consumed. These things didn't have to remain visible, they could also be kept in the soil of the sacred area. The deep well shafts were a perfectly obvious choice for convenient dumps.

During all excavations at Greek sanctuaries, archaeologists concentrated on the ruins of temples and the remnants of oblations. That the festival meadows received hardly any attention was simply due to the lack of traces above ground. Only the large and heavily frequented sanctuaries received a permanent infrastructure over the years.

In Olympia and other comparable sanctuaries the switch from temporary constructions to actual buildings began in the fourth century B.C. These were expanded and modified until the fourth century A.D. The Olympians built hostels (fig. 9, nos. 17 and 18), banquet pavilions (fig. 9, no. 19; fig. 15), shops (fig. 9, no. 20), and a large number of baths (fig. 9, nos. 19–23), which perhaps should be more aptly called "hygiene stations." For instance, they also included provisions for hair and skin care. We have already mentioned the fact that all these servicing stations were leased to private businessmen (see chapter 12).

When a permanent infrastructure was designed, the water supply system was one of its most crucial elements. It allows us to trace back how, from the fourth century B.C. on, the ever more pressing problem of supplying water was improved over the centuries. All existing water supply techniques were employed, from wells made of stones and cisterns to primitive clay pipes, to more sophisticated pressure pipes made of clay or lead, to an aqueduct that could carry larger amounts of water. What had long since become standard in Greek cities and many private houses was now also available to Olympia's visitors in the sanctuary's lodgings and installations: wells with water cascades, water fountains in the banquet rooms—and water closets (fig. 16)!

We will look at this more closely in later chapters. But first let us focus on a few installations one would not necessarily expect to find in a sanctuary, which however are still characteristic of Olympia's public image.

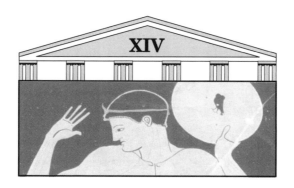

THE GYMNASIUM
AND ART EXHIBITS

To the south of the Temple of Zeus, already on the festival
meadow but at a prominent spot near the procession route, is a
building complex ancient sources call *bouleuterion* (city hall, see
fig. 9, no. 11). A square courtyard (c. 46 x 46 feet) forms the center of that compound. Adjacent to it, on the north and south
sides, are two halls measuring 36 x 72 feet each. Both halls are
open toward the east and have semicircular apses in the west.
This complex was not erected all at once. Its various parts were
built in the second half of the sixth century B.C. within a span
of three or four decades. In the fourth century B.C. a vestibule
was added to the three-part building, constituting yet another
example of a covered spectator stand, like the one that was discussed earlier (chapter 10) in connection with the so-called Echo
Portico.

When we had a closer look at the Temple of Zeus (above,
chapter 9), we found out about the custom of convening council
meetings in the sanctuaries. Hence it does not come as a surprise to hear that Olympia had a city hall. Yet the Bouleuterion
was probably not the meeting place of the council of Elis, rather
it served the sanctuary's needs. We know from numerous
inscriptions that there was an "Olympic Council," which must

have assembled in the Bouleuterion. It was one of the council's tasks to decide on whether or not to grant permission to erect a statue in the sanctuary.

In his description of Olympia, Pausanias has given us yet another indication of how the Bouleuterion was used:

> . . . the Zeus of the Council Chamber is of all the images of Zeus the one most likely to strike terror into the hearts of sinners. He is surnamed Oath-god, and in each hand he holds a thunderbolt. Beside this image it is the custom for athletes, their fathers and their brothers, as well as their trainers, to swear an oath upon slices of boar's flesh that in nothing will they sin against the Olympic games. The athletes take this further oath also, that for ten successive months they have strictly followed the regulations for training. An oath is also taken by those who examine the boys, or the foals entering for races, that they will decide fairly and without taking bribes, and that they will keep secret what they learn about a candidate, whether accepted or not.
>
> (Pausanias V 24, 9–10[1])

In other words, the large building complex may have served the Olympic Council for instruction and for administering oaths to the athletes and their attendants. In this connection we may ask ourselves if the open square did not serve as the place for the athletes' final preparations before a contest, until a special training hall was built for that purpose directly next to the venues in the fourth century B.C. (see chapter 11).

In the cities the city halls were not reserved for council meetings either. They were multipurpose rooms where, aside from political gatherings, cultural events took place as well. Yet in Olympia the Bouleuterion is never mentioned in this connection. Instead, we have learned (in chapter 9) that the Zeus Temple's back room (*opisthodom*) was sometimes used for cul-

---

1. Pausanias, *Description of Greece*, Book V: "Elis," in *Pausanias II*, tr. W. H. S. Jones and H. A. Ormerod, Loeb Classical Library 188 (Cambridge, Mass.: Harvard University Press, 1977; first printed in 1926), p. 529.

tural purposes. We will shortly hear about another location for such events.

Perhaps we can associate the Bouleuterion with another custom that is well documented for Greece's large sanctuaries of more than local interest. When official festival legations got together at the cult festival, they also used this opportunity to hold political talks and negotiations if necessary. The assembly, in 428 B.C., of the Peloponnesian League mentioned above (chapter 12) might well have taken place in one of the halls of the Bouleuterion.

Ancient sources mention an additional type of building we really find only in the cities: the so-called *prytaneion*, which served as an administrative office for the elected city council. Clearly the Prytaneion had a special significance for the community, as it was the location of the official state fireplace. On this altar—the Altar of Hestia—burned the "Eternal Flame," which provided the citizens with the fire they needed for their stoves at home.

When Olympia was taken over by the Eleians, they apparently transferred their Altar of Hestia to the Zeus sanctuary, as a consequence of which all citizens of Elis had to get their fire from Olympia. This was no doubt a deliberate act on their part to firmly link the sanctuary to its new lords. Using sacred values for power-political ends was nothing unusual in Greek cities.

By transferring the city's Prytaneion into the Zeus sanctuary, Elis officials were on the one hand pursuing political goals at home. Yet the administrative office in Olympia also served the Eleians to promote themselves in the eyes of the foreign visitors attending the festival. Thus we may justly call the Prytaneion the Eleians' official guest house, where the City of Elis held receptions during the cult festival, and where the Eleians invited the victorious athletes for the festival banquet concluding the Games.

Originally the Prytaneion was located at a representative spot in the southeastern part of the sanctuary, diagonally across from the Temple of Zeus (fig. 9, no. 9). After the victors were crowned in the Zeus Temple's vestibule, the reception guests had only a short walk to the big communal banquet room. At a date we can no longer precisely determine, but certainly in the first century A.D., the Prytaneion received a new location in the sanctuary's northwestern part (fig. 9, no. 10). The decisive reason for this may have been that the old location was too close to the overcrowded festival meadow, while the northwestern area was among the sacred precinct's most quiet and—thanks to the shade from the Hill of Cronus—most pleasant parts.

Among those of Olympia's facilities one would not automatically expect to find at a sanctuary was the *gymnasion*. Located in the sanctuary's western part, it consists of two architectural elements: one plaza, approximately 220 yards long and 100 yards wide and enclosed by halls (fig. 9, no. 15), and a smaller square whose sides measured about 72 yards each (fig. 9, no. 14; fig. 17).

The gymnasiums in Greek cities served the instruction of (male) youth. It is a well-known fact that this included a great deal of physical education besides intellectual instruction. Thus a *gymnasion* was a training site for athletic exercises, and so it does not seem out of place at Olympia. Still, we should not rashly assume that this elaborate installation was exclusively used in connection with the contests during the cult festival.

As we have seen (chapter 11), the athletes' actual preparation took place in the gymnasiums of the City of Elis. Contestants could warm up in the training hall directly by the Stadium, and previously perhaps in the Bouleuterion's courtyard. The athletes had a maximum of five days of continuous training, and only once every four years at that. To be sure, the sports arenas themselves were also built at great expense for just as brief a time period. Indeed, that the gymnasium was used only for brief periods is not the real reason why we should not assume that it was specially built for those who participated in the cult festival's contests.

We do not know for certain what the main purpose of the

square facility in the southern part of the complex was (fig. 9, no. 14; fig. 17). Obviously, the inner courtyard offered the heavy athletes everything they needed for their training. Since one of the rooms adjacent to the court was equipped as a lavatory (*loutron*), we cannot seriously doubt that it was indeed used for athletic exercises. Essentially, however, the square space contains rooms just like the ones in gymnasiums used for young people's intellectual instruction. The rooms of different sizes have rows of benches. These are the typical "lecture halls" in which orators, philosophers, and scholars in different fields gave their lectures to an audience that could discuss afterwards what it had heard. Recently one of the rooms in the court's west wing was identified as a banquet room. All this indicates that the building's primary function was outside the field of athletics.

Again we are reminded of the fact that not only athletes and sports fans attended the cult festival at Olympia. Greeks from all parts of the Mediterranean flocking together was such a unique event, it always also attracted people who tried to present their ideas and artistic achievements to the public. We have already mentioned that some took this opportunity to publicize their political views and philosophical ideas (chapter 8). Ancient sources also tell us that artists exhibited their works during the festival, and that they were personally present there: the painter Aëtion, for instance, achieved great success in Olympia with his painting *Alexander the Great's Wedding in Olympia* (Lucian, *Herodotus* 4); rhapsodes declaimed their poems (Diodorus XIV 109).

The square, colonnaded court with its adjacent halls was an appropriate setting for intellectual-cultural events of this kind. Yet this auditorium was not built until the early third century B.C. We may assume that for these purposes as well, there were temporary festival tents in the preceding centuries.

An important reason for the development of an infrastructure at Olympia that went far beyond what was absolutely necessary was that many Greeks put great stake in their public role as patrons and benefactors of this famous and much-frequented site.

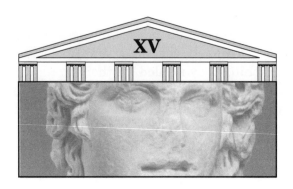

ALEXANDER THE GREAT AND OTHER BENEFACTORS

Greek sanctuaries were always institutions belonging to a political community that was of course responsible for maintaining and equipping the sacred area. The appearance of the communities' places of worship determined their public identity. Expensive oblations attested to the citizens' prosperity. Donations from foreigners were a tribute to a city's political significance.

If a sanctuary was very famous, however, there was also a reverse effect: every offering donated to the sanctuary was noticed by the site's numerous visitors. Thus it is not surprising that Olympia attracted a particularly large number of benefactors who wanted to effectively promote themselves. We are specifically referring to those benefactors who contributed financially to the improvement of Olympia's infrastructure.

The earliest benefactor of this kind whom scholars have been able to identify was a certain Leonides. Around the mid-fourth century B.C. he donated a building to the sanctuary that contained six banquet rooms, in addition to several apartments. It was called the Leonidaeon, after its donor (fig. 9, no. 17; fig. 15).

Fig. 16. Latrine with water closet, a rare privilege.

When a new building, the athletes' guild's clubhouse, was erected in the southwestern part of the sanctuary in the late first century A.D., a latrine accessible to the public was also part of the design. On three sides of the rectangular room a wood or stone construction provided seats for approximately fifteen people. In antiquity it was a matter of course that latrines were communal. They were popular places for communicating with others. The excrements piled up in the surrounding shaft that is well preserved to this day. A subterranean channel emptied the waste into the Alpheus. To relieve themselves, the vast majority of visitors went to the two rivers at the edge of the sanctuary anyway. Apart from the heat and the crowded conditions, the festivalgoers had to endure bad smells that are hardly conceivable for us today. This did not, however, make Olympia any less attractive.

We have already discussed the function of these dining rooms (chapter 13). With its measurements of approximately 82 x 89 yards (nearly 1.5 acres) this construction surpassed all other buildings in Olympia. A special attraction was probably the courtyard with its more than 7,500 square feet. Lined by columns like a cloister, and planted like a park, it was an oasis of quiet for visitors who needed a respite from the hubbub of the festival.

Obviously, a place like this was available only to a privileged few among the festival-goers. Still, even all those to whom this place was not accessible could get glimpses of the Leonidaeon's splendor, for Leonides had seen to it that a portico surrounded the entire building. Since it was located directly by the sanctuary entrance, all visitors approaching Olympia could see the west colonnade well before they arrived. Inside the place of worship, the main path led along the south colonnade toward the sanctuary's center.

As we have said, the building was named after its donor, who evidently was a wealthy man. Memory of him paled quickly, however. As early as the second century A.D., there was no longer any reliable information on the erstwhile benefactor. Pausanias called him a "local," that is to say, a citizen of Elis, but the remnants of the donor's inscription clearly indicate a man from the isle of Naxos in the Aegean Sea: *Leonides from Naxos, son of Leotos, erected this building and offered it to Zeus in Olympia.*

The wording of this inscription suggests that Leonides was also the architect of the building. It is possible that he is identical with the architect Leonides whom the ancient architecture historian Vitruvius mentioned in his major handbook (VII), where he is however counted among the "less famous" representatives of their trade. We do not know Leonides' motivation for donating such a magnificent banquet pavilion, but as a benefaction, erecting a building in a prominent place as proof of one's abilities, and of using this quite bluntly as publicity in order to acquire commissions, was perfectly in line with the customs of the time.

Contrary to donations from a private individual such as Leonides, we need not be hesitant about establishing the reasons behind the donations by politicians. By taking charge of important building projects, they supported the pertinent cities and won the citizens' favor. Efforts in that vein increased significantly in the second half of the fourth century B.C. The old system of autonomous city-states had exhausted itself in endless civil wars. This alerted the surrounding monarchies to compete for political power over as large parts of Greece as possible with a "carrot and a stick"—that is to say, with benefactions as well as merciless warfare.

The Greeks' neighbors in the north, the Macedonians, were the first to prevail. This was particularly painful to Greece, as its population had staunchly denied that Macedonians had Greek blood in their veins—they were considered barbarians. Notably Olympia, whose cult festival could be attended only by Greeks, had taken a clear stand on this issue: as late as the fifth century B.C. it wanted to deny the Macedonian King Alexander the Great the right to participate in the contests because he was "not Greek." More than a century later—after the battle of Chaeronea in 338 B.C.—Greece had to acknowledge Macedonia as its leader. The new power structure affected Olympia in two ways.

The Macedonians of course wanted to leave a visible mark of their triumph. King Philip II, their victorious commander, survived the battle for only a brief period. Thus it was left to his son and successor, Alexander the Great, to erect the monument of victory. It was at the same time a monument in honor and memory of his father and predecessor. Alexander chose the form of a round temple for this monument, which was called "Philippeion" after the king (fig. 9, no. 8). Such buildings were sights the Greeks were well acquainted with, but not in connection with the glorification of a military victory. They might erect round temples over the memorial sites of prominent ancestors, who were worshiped as heroes. Inside the round buildings were statues of the royal family, which were painted to look as though they were made of gold and ivory, like the one in the Temple of Zeus.

The Greeks must have considered the Philippeion an affront, especially since it was directly next to the age-old hero's grave of Pelops (fig. 9, no. 2). It seems, however, that the Macedonians did not simply mean to manifest their power in such a blunt way but also to make a genuine donation to the sanctuary. In any event, the same architect who designed the Philippeion was also involved in the plans for another building: the one-hundred-yard-long hall that marks the altar site's eastern border (fig. 9, no. 7).

Originally this was the site of the wall accommodating the spectators. As explained above (chapter 10), this wall had to be replaced by the training hall. The decision to make this change was made easier by the fact that this allowed the builders to remodel the *theatron*'s eastern spectator stand in the contemporary style. Modern stands were in the form of an oblong portico. From its covered inner court it was more comfortable to follow the events on the festival ground. The ostentatious colonnade obviously gave the festival ground itself a more impressive appearance. The sanctuary administration probably managed to get the Macedonians to sponsor the hall construction at that time—in any event, the decorations of the hall's foundation with its steps noticeably resemble those of the Philippeion.

The Macedonian royal court's involvement would also explain why construction of the hall stopped after the base was built, for after Alexander the Great's early death in 323 B.C. little time was left for cultural donations. As we know, a bitter fight about Alexander's succession ensued. The vast empire he had created, uniting Greece, Asia Minor, Persia, and Egypt—to mention only the most important territories—crumbled. Every monarchy that had come about as a result of this collapse tried to reunite and lead the huge empire. Countries and cities often took advantage of this rivalry, as everyone wooed them.

After Alexander's death, the Macedonians turned from benefactors to transgressors in Olympia. In 312 B.C. one of their
leaders (Telesphorus, a nephew of the diadochus Antigonus I)
plundered the sanctuary in order to fill his war chest. This gave
members of another dynasty the opportunity to present themselves to their best advantage: King Ptolemy I compensated the
sanctuary for its losses.

The dynasty of the Ptolemies was seated in Alexandria, the
metropolis Alexander had founded in the Nile delta. In the early
third century B.C. the Ptolemies were the Macedonians' most
serious rivals in the fight for predominance in Greece. Their
conduct in Olympia was less obtrusive and much more effective
than Macedonia's.

The Ptolemaean dynasty was also represented with statues
in Olympia, but contrary to the Macedonians, the Ptolemies did
not choose the arrogant form of cultic self-glorification. In fact,
at least officially they were not even involved in the donation of
the monument in their honor, which was commissioned by the
commander of their fleet and expressed his reverence for his
lord Ptolemy II and the king's wife and co-regent Arsinoë before
the eyes of the world that was gathered at Olympia around 270
B.C. It is an unusual monument: on a sixty-five-foot-long pedestal a thirty-foot-tall column was erected in each corner, on
which the statues of the king and queen were placed.

Shape and location of the Ptolemaean oblation were hardly a
matter of coincidence. They are a snide comment of sorts on the
unpopular Macedonians, for the oblong monument is directly in
front of the empty structure with its completed steps that originally was to be the foundation of the hall the Macedonians had
promised! Those admiring the impressive Ptolemaean monument automatically also saw the embarrassing construction
hole the Macedonians had left behind it. Now the Greeks gath-
ering in Olympia could judge for themselves who was deserving
of their trust.

Recent research has produced evidence that strongly suggests that the Ptolemaean dynasty also donated a famous build-

Fig. 17. The classrooms in Olympia's Palaestra.

In the cities of Greece, the Palaestra served approximately the same purpose as today's schools. Since physical education played a crucial part in ancient Greece, the Palaestra was also a place for sports. The center courtyard (illustration, right) was suitable for this. An essential part of all Greek Palaestras, however, were the rooms where the youths' intellectual education took place. In this photograph we see such "auditoriums," in the eastern wing of Olympia's Palaestra. Here is where prominent philosophers and scholars made their appearances during the cult festival and where artists exhibited their work. To a large extent the Olympic festival owed its excellent reputation to the cultural part of its program.

ing in Olympia. There are serious indications that Ptolemy II donated the Palaestra in the western part of the sacred precinct (fig. 9, no. 14; fig. 17).

In the second and first centuries B.C. Greece had suffered greatly through warfare and public humiliations. The battle over predominance in the Mediterranean became fiercer and fiercer, and the appearance of marauding pirate gangs made the conflicts ever more merciless. Even though the Romans ultimately pacified the region, they bore the major responsibility for the Greek cities' hard lot. Above all, they did take their independence away from them.

Two Roman commanders have even become synonymous with Greece's humiliation: Mummius, who commanded the army destroying Corinth (146 B.C.), and Sulla, who in the 80s B.C. systematically stole artifacts from Greek sanctuaries to pay his soldiers from the profit made on selling them.

Coming across these two names in a chapter on Olympia's benefactors may seem odd. Yet if we are to judge these men dispassionately, they cannot go unmentioned here. It is a historic fact that Mummius put a temporary end to the history of the City of Corinth in 146 B.C. On the other hand, there is also proof that he did so on strict orders from the Roman senate, against his personal conviction, and that he kept the destruction and pillaging that had been ordered to a minimum. The Corinthians' civil rights were abolished at the time, and the city's main buildings therefore completely razed.

After his military action in Corinth, Mummius traveled through the entire country to pay reverence to the Greeks by erecting statues in many sanctuaries. Olympia, too, was among the recipients of these gifts. Apparently the Greeks were relieved that the general, rather than acting as a merciless conqueror, instead became involved in their sanctuaries, donating oblations just as if he were a Greek himself. Olympia—as well as other cities—expressed their gratitude by erecting statues in his honor. What was important for the Greeks was the realization that while the Romans may have been their enemies on the battlefield, they still manifested their appreciation and admiration of Greek culture.

And what about Sulla? He fully deserves the stigma as the pillager of Greek sanctuaries that is attached to his name. Like many others before him—Greeks too—he paid his soldiers mainly by raiding temples' chests. Still, we get a full picture of him only if we also consider his subsequent actions. As soon as it was politically feasible, he saw to it that the three sanctuaries whose treasuries he had plundered (aside from Olympia, Delphi, and Epidaurus) were compensated for their losses. He took on a long drawn-out battle on this behalf against Rome's finance department, seeing the matter through the entire appeals process. Sulla certainly was not a benefactor who enriched Olympia the way the private individual Leonides or King Ptolemy II had. Still, the cliché of the raving mad robber who had no respect for the Greek gods and almost ruined the sanctuary can no longer be sustained.

The erection in the first century B.C. of a magnificent portal for the *gymnasion* also defies the popular view of the sanctuary's decline around that time. It, too, was probably the gift of a benefactor, whose identity however is still a mystery.

The Emperor Augustus was an admirer of Greek culture. He was mainly interested in the golden age of philosophy and art. He did, however, have difficulty dealing with contemporary Greeks, as he held a grudge against them for so obstinately supporting the party of his adversary Marc Antony during Rome's civil war. He visited Athens only briefly on his travels, and Olympia not at all. Therefore, he was only an indirect benefactor at Olympia. In his stead, two men from among his inner circle became active in this respect. One was his son-in-law and designated successor, Agrippa, and the other was the man who in the Christian Western world became known as the children's murderer of Bethlehem, King Herod of Judea.

Two buildings were erected in Olympia during the years these two men strove to embellish the sanctuary. Bath facilities in the contemporary style, located west of the administration building (fig. 9, no. 16), may have been a donation by Herod, who admired Western culture, for there is a very similar building in the fortress of Masada, which he had erected.

Yet there was another building that was more spectacular. It makes us revisit the fate of the hall east of the altar site. Three hundred years after construction of the hall most likely initiated by Alexander the Great, the building that had been planned was added to the finished pedestal after all. This hall, commonly called Echo Portico or Echo Stoa, had originally been planned as a spectator stand but could fulfill its original purpose only to a limited degree, as the front side had meanwhile been filled with oblations. Yet the hall was probably completed less out of practical considerations than for nostalgic reasons, to cherish the sentimental memory of Greece's former glory, now long gone. Needless to say, the two possible donors—Herod and Agrippa—also must have been thrilled to finish a building in honor of King Augustus that had once been begun by Alexander the Great. Being thus regarded as the "New Alexander," Augustus was bound to be flattered.

In our discussion of the great donations for the Zeus sanctuary, we have so far only mentioned successful *men* from the world of economy and politics. Considering how entirely men dominated the Greek and Roman world, it is hard to imagine how women might have distinguished themselves in a similar manner. It is all the more surprising that as yet, scholars have consistently ignored concrete evidence of a benefactress in Olympia.

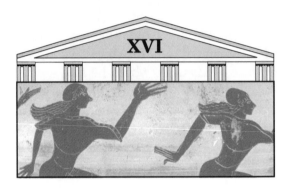

THIRST FOR OLYMPIA

At the cult festival of A.D. 153, a prominent woman had the honor of occupying the seat of Demeter-Chamyne in the Olympic Stadium. Her name was Regilla. A Roman by birth, she was married to the arguably most famous Greek of the time, Herodes Atticus.

Herodes Atticus was a member of a Greek family whose ancestral home lay in a place fraught with history: Marathon. His ancestors had accumulated a vast fortune, and the family's expansive estates were extremely profitable. Yet its wealth was tarnished inasmuch as Herodes' father was strongly suspected of having increased his fortune by dishonest means. His official version was that he had found a treasure that was buried on his property. Herodes received a good education at the Philosophical School in Athens. He had the obligatory sequence of administrative positions, eventually assuming the highest posts of political and ecclesiastical life in Athens.

As was customary at the time, Herodes established close contacts with Rome, the center of the empire, of which Greece was then a province (called Achaea). In Rome he again climbed all the way up the ladder of a political career, which ultimately gave him direct access to the imperial court. It was there that he met a certain Annia Regilla, whom he married soon there-

Fig. 18. Waterworks in honor of the fertility goddess Demeter.
    The worship of numerous fertility goddesses was among the oldest rites at
Olympia. Demeter was part of that divine group. Hardly any Greek deity
enjoyed such lasting popularity as she did. Even during the period of the
Roman Empire, women from the leading families applied for the office of
priestess of Demeter. Regilla donated an expensive fountain display as
thanks for being appointed to that post. The semicircular edge of the fountain
simultaneously served as a base for two galleries of statues.

after. When Herodes returned to his Greek home in the middle
of the second century A.D., he and his wife Regilla embodied the
very concept of blending Greek and Roman accomplishments
and traditions.

They held on to this idea even after they had settled in
Athens. Regilla assumed distinguished posts in Greek religious
life. Her election as Demeter's priestess in Olympia was a special honor and no doubt marked the epitome of her and her hus-
band's ideals. This motivated them to jointly leave a lasting
memorial in the sanctuary.

Their donation continued to be useful to all visitors of the
sanctuary even after their death: they conducted water to
Olympia from a spring some four miles away. It is documented
that Herodes himself donated the water pipes. The priestess of
Demeter, Regilla, embellished the donation by adding a magnificent fountain in the center of the sanctuary. At the southern
slopes of the Hill of Cronus, on the Treasury Terrace (fig. 9, no.
6; fig. 18), it seemed convenient to let the water cascade through
several basins down into the Altis.

A magnificent thirty-foot-high façade rose above the upper-
most semicircular basin of this twenty-three-foot-high work of
water art. Spread over two floors, this display wall contained
twenty-two round niches in which were placed altogether twenty-six life-size statues. The two galleries of statues, in turn, represented two different oblations. Once again Herodes Atticus
was one of the donors. He had statues of members of the Roman
imperial family put in the niches on the lower floor. The center
niche was reserved for Zeus, the lord of the sanctuary. The
Eleians, recipients of such abundant presents from Herodes
and Regilla, expressed their thanks by putting statues of members of the benefactors' family in the upper row of niches. The
figure of the god that once occupied this gallery's center niche
was destroyed. We are inclined to assume that within the context of this complex oblation was a statue of the goddess to
whose service the donator Regilla had devoted herself:
Demeter-Chamyne.

It is impossible to overlook the mix of Greek and Roman elements in this valuable oblation, which makes it fit snugly into
the traditional series of politically motivated offerings we have
repeatedly mentioned. That the oblation is associated with the
politician Herodes Atticus' name not only today, but carried his
name even in antiquity, is no coincidence. Yet the work's traditional name, "Nymphaeum of Herodes Atticus," fails to
acknowledge Regilla's crucial contribution.

Needless to say, as priestess of Demeter, honoring the age-old
cult of this goddess was important to her. If life-giving water
alone is a fitting enough element to honor the vegetation goddess Demeter, the choice of location could not have been more
appropriate for an offering to Demeter. Since the days of old, the
hollow between the Cronus Hill and the Gaion had contained
places of worship for goddesses (see chapter 2). The fountain,
built in the second century A.D., reminded visitors of the sanctuary's origins. Once again we can recognize the Greeks' respect
for ancient places of worship, just as we noticed earlier when
taking a closer look at the Stadium.

Right after the dedication of the fountain, while the cult festival of A.D. 153 was still underway, a peculiar incident happened in Olympia. One of the philosophers who, as we have
seen, were among the festival's regular visitors, attracted a
large audience in the middle of the sanctuary. He vociferously
bemoaned Olympia's decline. His complaint was that the sanctuary administration had allowed the festival to completely
change its character. Those, he said, who came to Olympia in
former days used to know that they were in danger of dying of
thirst. Indeed, more than a few people had fallen victim to the
heat, dust, and draught in the past. Those who had not survived
Olympia were surely not worth mourning over. Now, however,
that constantly running spring water was being conducted into
the sanctuary, this form of selection had been abolished, and
therefore the festival attendants were being perversely molly-
coddled.

It is obvious that such a provocative speech could only come

from the mouth of a Cynic philosopher. Peregrinus, a native of
Asia Minor, was well known for his diatribes. In Olympia, he
clearly overdid it—for while he was speaking, he himself chose
to enjoy sipping from the refreshing water. The spectators were
so indignant that they would have stoned Peregrinus had he
not managed to find refuge at the Altar of Zeus at the last
minute.

Peregrinus was not the only one whose sojourn at Olympia is
described with obvious disgust in ancient sources.

EMPEROR NERO
AT OLYMPIA

Whenever tourist groups are guided through Olympia today, one can always hear roaring laughter in the southeastern part of the sanctuary. Invariably they are just being told how Nero used to compete in the races with his ten-horse chariot, how he was hurled out of his chariot, only to have himself—numb both from the fall and the flush of victory—declared the glorious winner of the race. The cue "Nero" is dropped on that particular part of the tour through the sanctuary because the disgrace caused by Nero seems to be palpable there. In any event, the remains of what clearly used to be brick buildings in the style fashionable in the era of Roman emperors are called "House of Nero" on the maps and in the travel guides.

Nero did visit Olympia. There are more ancient sources documenting his sojourn there than for almost any other visitor. Still, finding out what really happened during his visit is a most difficult task.

Historians have long since realized that the ancient authors (Suetonius, Cassius Dio) from whom we have our knowledge of Nero's trip to Greece are by no means reliable reporters. Both lived after Nero's death and, therefore, had to base their accounts on earlier documents. We know the authors they consulted: Pliny the Older, Cluvius Rufus, and Fabius Rusticus. None of them viewed Nero dispassionately. Either they were his fierce political enemies, or they were his former companions who did not pull their punches after Nero's death, if only to save their own skin. To be sure, we must not categorically deny that there is some truth to their reports. Still, there can be no doubt that they did present a very lopsided picture of Nero.

We may expect such distortions especially in those passages in which Nero's relationship with Greek culture is portrayed, for one of the reasons that particular Roman emperor was considered such a dubious character was the downright unbridled passion he felt for all matters Greek. Rome was especially alarmed by the danger—which became more and more urgent— of the emperor shifting central control over the Roman Empire from Rome to somewhere in Greece. The old metropolis Alexandria seemed like a strong possibility. Nero was by no means the first Roman emperor playing with this idea, but he pushed it as none of his predecessors ever had.

Nero spoke Greek, knew the Homeric Hymns by heart, surrounded himself with Greek advisers, and built a *gymnasion* in the Greek style in Rome. It is obvious that the upper class in ancient Rome viewed this with great suspicion and ridiculed it in front of the Roman people. Keeping all this in mind, we do have to be extremely skeptical about the reports on Nero's appearance at Olympia.

More recently, historians have found a new approach to an understanding of Nero's sojourn in Greece. For one thing, by analyzing various inscriptions and for the first time examining highly informative coins, they were able to reconstruct his trip much more precisely than before. This alone lets us see Nero's trip in a radically different light. The assumption that Nero was running from one Greek venue to a next like a maniac in order to let himself be carried away by his victories—all of them fixed in advance—can no longer be sustained.

In the fall of A.D. 66 Nero, along with a huge retinue and some 5,000 soldiers, embarked on his journey to Greece. He was headed for Alexandria and planning to take off from there on an expedition to the Arabian peninsula—an expedition Alexander the Great had begun four hundred years before him but been unable to complete. From the start Nero intended to stop over in Corinth, the capital of the Roman province of Achaea, which comprised Central Greece and the Peloponnesus. He wanted to express his admiration of Greek culture at the Poseidon sanctuary directly next to Corinth by giving back their independence to the Central Greek cities and the Peloponnesus. In November 66 he actually did realize his intent in a festive proclamation. An inscription in Epidaurus documents that the Greek cities immediately began with the administrative restructuring this step entailed.

It was an old tradition in Greece to honor benefactors by, among other things, inviting them to famous cult festivals, which as an additional honor were rescheduled if necessary. Nero, too, was a benefactor who traveled through the former province of his, which he had released into independence. The cities he visited stamped coins commemorating his declaration of independence. Corinth, Argos, Nemea, Delphi, Actium, and of course Olympia are documented in this manner as stops on this trip of honor.

We do not know what Nero actually did at the cities and sanctuaries he visited and should speculate about it with caution. There is a possible indication that his appearance was not out of line but that he may have conducted himself appropriately for the festive occasion that a reception for illustrious visitors like him was: only a few decades after Nero's reign, a prominent Greek, discussing the conditions in his home country, keyed in on the situation at the sanctuaries at the beginning of the second century A.D. It was the philosopher and writer Plutarch, who at some point had been a priest at Delphi. While Plutarch reported many violations of the dignity of the sacred sites in Greece, he did not utter a single negative word on Nero in this context!

Surely Nero was not responsible for two things. One was the

erection of a palace for him opposite the Temple of Zeus. Closer examination of the excavation logs does not even clearly tell us if the so-called "House of Nero" was built during his reign. We only know for certain that some of the construction took place during the second and third centuries. Yet even if construction had started while he was emperor, we have no idea whatsoever as to the building's supposed purpose.

A second "acquittal" is also in order regarding the charge that Nero had to a large extent destroyed or appropriated statues. According to sources not on Olympia but on two other places in Greece, Nero, like many other Roman art connoisseurs, wanted to acquire Greek statues. His art agents initiated negotiations. Nero's request was denied. The cities he had approached refused to sell the statues he had requested, and the emperor respected that decision.

Now the most recent excavations have unearthed another track leading to Nero, at an entirely different spot in the sanctuary. In the last few years a building was excavated in the southwestern corner of the part of the ancient area that can be seen today (fig. 9, no. 24). It is possible both to date this building and determine its purpose with some precision. It was used by the members of the parent organization of the Greek athletes' guilds (fig. 19).

The athletic associations served to improve the organization of athletic contests and to provide for the aged athletes. One of these associations' main tasks was to see to the observation of the strict contest rules. To become members, candidates had to pass an examination of their ethical and moral backgrounds. The patron saint of the athletes' guilds was Hercules. Their places of assembly and official personnel were organized after the Hercules sanctuaries. The notion that the athletic associations had undermined the sacred nature of the competitions in Greek sanctuaries could not be further from the truth.

The architectural history of the newly excavated athletes' guild's building is interesting. The lower part of the stonework exhibits a so-called "reticulate" construction technique with

Fig. 19. The clubhouse of the athletes' guild from the late first century A.D.
The athletes revered Hercules as their patron, and the building is dedicated to him. The construction was begun with the support of Emperor Nero, who was a great admirer and sponsor of Greek athletes. In front of the façade, which was clad with marble and decorated with statues, was a courtyard surrounded by pillars. The two large rooms on the sides of the courtyard served as training rooms for wrestlers and weight-lifters.

Fig. 20. A bronze inscription from the clubhouse of
the athletes' guild shows that the cult festival continued along with the competitions until A.D. 385.
Until this discovery, the complete list of Olympic
champions names' had ended with the year 277.

which we are familiar from Rome. Stones with a square surface area are put together in such a way that the seams run diagonally, thus forming a mesh pattern. The walls at Olympia are built in a meticulous way that we know of only from the best buildings in Rome itself. The only explanation for this is that masons from Rome were hired for this job.

We know of the employment of masonic lodges from the City of Rome outside of Rome only in cases where construction had been ordered by the emperor himself. Since excavations have allowed us to determine that construction of the clubhouse began at the time of Nero's rule, we can identify Nero as the founder of the installation.

The Roman workers could stay in Olympia for only a short while. The stonework they raised comes to an abrupt halt. This allows us to reconstruct with considerable likelihood the following sequence of events: On the occasion of his visit at Olympia in the winter of 66–67, the emperor and the sanctuary administration agreed on the construction of a building Olympia urgently needed for the local representation of the athletes' guilds. Construction is prepared and finally begun in A.D. 67. Yet only a short while later, in early 68, there was a conspiracy against Nero in Rome, which caused him to cancel his already delayed trip to Alexandria and also to cut short his stay in Greece. Once back in Rome, Nero had to recognize that he was politically isolated. In June of that same year he committed suicide.

At that point at the latest, the Roman masons Nero had sent to Olympia and financed left the construction site. That the few walls that were already raised were not torn down in contempt for the toppled emperor is an indication that the sanctuary administration and Nero were on good terms. Rather, construction of the building, for which there seems to have been an urgent need, was quickly finished with the help of new sponsors. The building was used until the end of the fourth century A.D. A recently found bronze inscription on the building (fig. 20) documents the presence of Olympic champions until A.D. 385.

The last name to be entered was that of Zopyrus, a boxer from Athens.

Basically, the athletes' guilds were very conservative institutions. Since their internal organization followed strict rules, they were probably indispensable for upholding the sound condition Olympia was in, until the majority of people in the Alpheus Valley decided in the late fourth century A.D. to convert to Christianity.

AN HONORABLE END

Their incorporation into the Roman Empire sealed the Greek cities' fate politically. Still, the Greek settlements received special treatment among all Roman provinces. The Romans had a tremendous appreciation of Greek culture. From their direct exposure to Greek art and thought, they had a thorough understanding of it, and without the Romans' commitment to Greek culture, we would not possess as many great ancient texts and paintings as we do today.

Olympia, too, profited from Rome's predisposition toward all things Greek. The oblation by Herodes Atticus and Regilla discussed above, in which Greek gods, Roman emperors, and the Greco-Roman family of the donors appear next to each other, is an obvious symbol of this positive development.

In this connection we should point out another family's activities. The family is less prominent than the former, but its efforts on behalf of Olympia were perhaps even more effective. It also has a mix of Greek and Roman elements. We are speaking of the Vettulenis, who had probably emigrated to Greece as early as the second or first century B.C. so as to have a more convenient basis for their tradings between Greece and Central Italy.

One branch of the family settled in Elis. We can trace the

Vettulenis' efforts on behalf of the Zeus sanctuary over a period of two-hundred years. Some members of the clan took part in the athletic contests—and successfully at that. Others became priests. A certain Lucius Vettulenus Laetus was among the group of eminent benefactors. It is probably due to his efforts that the athletes' guilds' clubhouse discussed in the previous chapter was completed after Nero's death. During excavations a few years ago, we discovered several fragments of a marble plate with an inscription mentioning Emperor Domitian as benefactor. There are many indications that this inscription, made in the summer of A.D. 84, refers to our building. It seems that Lucius Vettulenus Laetus was able to convince Emperor Domitian to finish the work Nero had begun. When the cult festival and its athletic contests were held at the Zeus sanctuary in the following year (A.D. 85), the athletes who had made the trip to Olympia enjoyed for the first time the advantages of a stately clubhouse. They honored their benefactor Lucius Vettulenus Laetus by erecting a statue of him.

Greeks and Romans took care of the maintenance of Olympia together. They joined in their appreciation of Greek athleticism, whose main location Olympia had remained even during that historic period.

Current excavations at Olympia produce ever more proof of the continued good internal and external condition of the Zeus sanctuary during the last centuries of its existence. On occasion the installations of the site's infrastructure, discussed in chapter 13, were maintained and modernized, that is to say, they were technologically as well as aesthetically brought up to current standards.

As during the previous centuries, the Zeus sanctuary was repeatedly hit by earthquakes during the period of the Roman Empire. A quake around A.D. 290 caused particularly great damage. As far as it affected the buildings, these were repaired. The government spared neither cost nor effort to have stonemasons and sculptors restore even the ornaments of the badly damaged marble roof of the Temple of Zeus.

That natural catastrophe did not diminish the influx of people. Around the turn of the fourth century A.D. the number of hygiene stations even had to be increased yet again. Thus still another bathhouse was built between the Leonidaeon and the athletes' clubhouse (fig. 9, no. 23). The sanctuary managed to commission an architect for this project who had developed an entirely new heating system for the baths.

Yet the earthquake of the late third century, from which Olympia seems to have recovered fairly quickly, had aftereffects that were to trouble the sanctuary greatly during the subsequent decades. Apparently the quay of the Cladeus had been damaged as well. In any event, the western part of the sanctuary was plagued by ever more frequent floods.

All these floods no doubt put a tremendous strain on the sanctuary administration, but they could be dealt with by way of technological improvements. Another challenge during that period was infinitely greater: Who in the fourth century A.D. was at all still interested in maintaining the Greek gods' old places of worship? Many people had long since turned to other religious movements. For instance, there were followers of the Anatolian savior Mithras or of the Egyptian religion's Isis. More and more people were also attracted by Christian ideas. Of the ancient Greek circle of gods, only the mystery cult of Demeter was able to maintain a continuous crowd of followers. People also still put their hope in the demigod Hercules. Many formerly significant places of worship, such as the Apollo sanctuary on Delos, an island in the Cyclades group, had closed their gates way back during the early years of the Roman Empire. The Apollo sanctuary in Delphi, too, had a serious crisis during the second century A.D.

Yet the existence of the ancient Greek places of worship was threatened not merely for religious reasons. We have seen (above, chapter 12) to what a large degree Greece's sanctuaries were an integral part of the country's social and cultural life. This vested the sanctuaries with great political significance in the world of ancient Greek states. Within the legal and political system of the Roman Empire, however, the sanctuaries had lost that role—in part, they even could disturb its order. Insisting on their traditional privileges would put the priests in conflict with the machinery of power in Rome.

During the fourth century A.D., after most of the Roman emperors had made their decision in favor of Christianity, the followers of Greek religions could easily be suspected of trying to politically oppose the emperor—which probably was often indeed the case. Now the fate of the sanctuaries depended mainly on the diplomatic skills of their priests.

In the critical years of Emperor Theodosius I's reign (379–95) Olympia seems to have been administrated by a circumspect committee of men. It is most certainly possible that the cult festival at Olympia, which was popular in the entire Mediterranean, was celebrated as a major cultural event the emperors could tolerate without any qualms. Theodosius did order all places of worship still in existence closed in A.D. 391, but it seems that Olympia was exempt from the mandate. From what our most recent excavations have brought to light, Olympia seems to have continued its cult-related operations until the first decades of the fifth century. It is likely that it submitted only to a second prohibition, decreed by Theodosius II (A.D. 402–50).

The sanctuary seems to have been dissolved peacefully. The plane at the foot of the Hill of Cronus again filled with life for another one hundred and fifty years, but it took on an entirely new meaning. By no means did the sanctuary's buildings, which had lost their purpose within a culture now gone, provide the people in the area with free construction material. Rather, after it had accumulated for centuries, the material was now used for a different end. The old place of worship turned into a settlement inhabited by Christians. The people who built their houses and workplaces there were, of course, attracted by the ideal conditions the sanctuary's former infrastructure offered them. The extensive water main system in particular must have been attractive to the new settlers. Some of the buildings could easi-

Fig. 21. Baths for a guesthouse around A.D. *300.*

Olympia was struck by a serious earthquake in the late third century A.D. This did not diminish the Olympic cult festival's attraction for visitors. Consequently, not only were the damages repaired, but new, additional buildings were erected to accommodate the festival attendants. An architect even developed a new form of heating for the small bath in the southwestern part of the sanctuary: he installed the heating pipes inside the walls.

Fig. 22. Winepress in the early Byzantine settlement.

During the first half of the fifth century A.D. the majority of Greeks turned toward Christianity. In the course of this development Olympia's Zeus sanctuary had to close its gates as well. Still, the numerous buildings did not remain useless. The small baths with their premises in the southwestern part of the sanctuary (fig. 21) were ideally suited for a winepress. Therefore a vintner remodeled the building for his purposes. A basin in which the grapes were pressed (by stomping) was put above the ancient mosaic floor. The juices expressed were stored in the adjoining room and fermented into wine.

Fig. 23. The Christian church in the early Byzantine settlement.
Unlike other Greek sanctuaries, in Olympia the temple was not turned into a Christian church. Instead, the Christians tried to find a large hall among the many structures, which they then slightly remodeled into a room suitable for their religious ceremonies.

ly be remodeled for their new purpose. The small bath facilities in the southwest, for instance, that were installed around A.D. 300 (fig. 9, no. 23), provided exactly the space needed for a wine-press (figs. 21 and 22). Thus one of the many vintners among those members of the community who had their own businesses and are historically documented settled there.

Aside from farming, which had always been important in the Alpheus Valley (chapter 2), a great variety of businesses contributed to the prosperity of the quickly growing settlement. Several potters, a number of smiths, and even a bone cutter who produced combs are documented. According to the most recent research, the area's pottery indicates that like the former sanctuary, the new settlement had an impact beyond the area's local borders. The people living there were in contact with the major trade centers in the Aegean.

Naturally, those settlers who had converted to Christianity also established a place for their religious celebrations. It is worthy of note that contrary to other places, the church was not moved into the former temple. Instead, a hall in the former administration complex was chosen for its site (fig. 9, no. 16; fig. 23). The latest research has discovered that this impressive church was established and furbished in the mid-fifth century.

The pagan temple continued to stand within sight of the Christian church, but it had been deprived of its former magnificence. It was now part of a fortress-like square of walls that enclosed the area from the Temple of Zeus to the large hall some 250 feet to the south (fig. 24). According to the latest findings, this little fortress was not erected as early as was assumed only a few years ago: it was not built in the third century A.D. but constituted part of the early Byzantine settlement. Yet what was its function?

Numerous enemy armies and looters invaded the south of Greece from the late fourth century A.D. on. Around A.D. 395 Alaric's Visigoths advanced to the area near Olympia. Around 470 the Vandals under their military commander Gaiseric, coming from Carthage, passed before the west coast of the

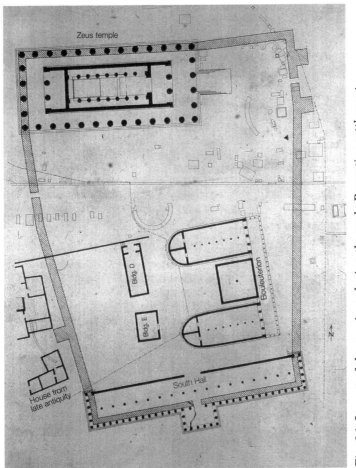

Fig. 24. Layout of the garrison during the early Byzantine settlement.

When the area of the sanctuary was turned into a settlement inhabited by work-men and vintners, the Temple of Zeus remained untouched. A high wall was built around it as well as a few other buildings in the area, turning it into a fortress of sorts. It is, however, also possible that it was the settlers' intention to protect mon-uments from among the former sanctuary's cultural assets inside the walled-in area.

Peloponnesus. Around 580, finally, the Avars and Slavs were advancing from the north. The bulwark was not large enough to serve either as a garrison for soldiers or as a refugee camp, nor was there a cistern, which would have been absolutely essential for these purposes. Material goods, however, could be safeguarded inside the walls. Three premises, left from the sanctuary period, were suitable for this: the former Temple of Zeus in the north, one of the Bouleuterion's two assembly halls in the center, and the long building containing several halls in the south. This offered sufficient storage room to get valuable goods out of harm's way or to store emergency food supplies.

Yet this may not have been the only purpose of the enclosure. The description by the first excavators in the nineteenth century indicates that the entry in the east was a sophisticated construction made of marble blocks. People would hardly have put such effort into this if the wall had been raised solely for emergencies. Apparently the gate was to give a dignified impression to those entering through it, as if they had to be prepared for the sight of the venerable Temple of Zeus that lay waiting for them. Indeed, instructions from Theodosius I's collection of statues have been preserved that direct the governors and inhabitants of the area to treat what was left behind from the Greco-Roman culture with respect. Thus many of the artifacts originally dedicated to pagan gods survived the change of religions. Some squares in the empire's capital, Constantinople, were veritable museums housing famous monuments from the heathen past. The wall enclosure around Olympia's Temple of Zeus also may have held some of the famed old statues from the sanctuary's supply.

Theodosius and the early Byzantine emperors were not necessarily admirers of ancient art, however. They may have protected the old buildings and statues for their material value: if need be, new coins could be made from melting down a bronze statue, for instance. It is also possible that Olympia's walls served as an imperial material depot. The latest excavations at Olympia have not only given us new insights into the sanctuary's history but have also sharpened our eye for the questions that future research will have to answer.

The last inhabitants of the settlement in the former Zeus sanctuary moved out of their homes in the early seventh century A.D. Some had left even back in the mid-sixth century. There were two reasons for this. One, living so close to the coast, which formed the border of the Eastern Roman Empire, did have its dangers. Yet the main reasons for leaving the area were probably imposed by nature: two big earthquakes around A.D. 522 and around 551, an outbreak of the plague sometime between A.D. 530 and 540, and finally, the regularly occurring floods of the Cladeus made life there unbearable. Worn down by these hardships, people left. Some buried their tools and even their money, clearly believing they would one day return—but their hopes did not come true. The last evidence of human life in the settlement are coins of Emperor Phocas (602–10).

After people had left, it took the Cladeus less than two hundred years to cover the plain at the foot of the Hill of Cronus, including the remains of the sanctuary and settlement, with a layer of sand thirteen to sixteen feet thick. When the Slavs took over the land a short time later, they also avoided the plain by the river, settling north of the Hill of Cronus in the shallow hills of the Cladeus Valley.

HISTORICAL OVERVIEW

I. SECULAR PRELUDE

2500–1900 B.C.: Settlement in the hilly area between the Hill of Cronus and the Alpheus bed. It is most likely the floods of the Cladeus river that force the inhabitants to leave their homes and to settle outside of this inhospitable area.

2nd millennium: After the settlement has been abandoned, the land is probably used for farming.

II. HISTORY OF THE SANCTUARY

11th century B.C.: The people living in the Alpheus Valley and the fertile, hilly land to the south establish a place of worship for the vegetation goddess Gaia on an isolated elevation at the foot of the Hill of Cronus. Possibly an oracle was connected to it next to a crevice.

10th century B.C.: Zeus becomes the center of cultic worship. His altar is made the site of the oracle, whose seers dispense advice in matters of warfare. The local hero Pelops is worshipped at his alleged grave. The original fertility cult is continued at the altars of Demeter, Aphrodite, and Artemis.

Late 8th century B.C.: A member of the Olympian family of seers accompanies the Peloponnesian émigrés to Sicily, contributing to their success in founding Syracuse. The colonists make their first thank-offerings (mainly war booty) to Olympia's helpful oracle site.

c. 700 B.C.: The cult festival at Olympia becomes the link between the colonists in the west and the Greek motherland. As a consequence, the sacred area is expanded. In this connection a stadium is built.

7th century B.C.: The athletic contests held as part of the cult festival attract more and more athletes from all over wherever there are Greek settlements. In order to store the numerous votive offerings (largely arms and armors from war booty), treasuries (constructions made of wood and clay, adorned with bronze reliefs) are built.

c. 600 B.C.: As lords of the sanctuary, the people in the hilly land south of the Alpheus construct their first temple (originally perhaps in honor of Zeus, later definitely dedicated to Hera).

c. 580 B.C.: The Eleians conquer the valley of the Alpheus and become the new lords of Olympia. This does not affect the activities of the oracle or the cult festival and its athletic contests.

6th and early 5th centuries B.C.: In quick succession, new treasuries are built, now made of stone, to store the continuous flow of oblations, most of which come from colonial cities in Lower Italy.

479 B.C.: Greece defeats Persia in a battle near Plataea. An Olympian seer is present to dispense advice.

476 B.C.: The first Olympian cult festival after the victory over Persia turns into a victory celebration. Festival attendants pray for harmony among all Greeks. Olympia becomes the seat of a Panhellenic arbitration court. This enhances the sanctuary's prestige, which in turn leads to major construction: the Eleians erect a temple in honor of Zeus (simultaneously the old Triphylian temple may have been rededicated to Hera). In the eastern part of the area, the festival site around the Altar of Zeus, embankments of earth are built to accommodate the spectators. The Stadium is therefore shifted further to the east. At the same time its stands are raised. The cult festival is extended into a five-day event.

457–456 B.C.: The Temple of Zeus is basically completed. The Panhellenic arbitration court has already lost its former jurisdiction. Following internal wars among the Greeks, more victory monuments than ever are erected in the sanctuary.

c. 430 B.C.: On a commission from Elis, Phidias is working on an almost forty-foot-high statue of Zeus, a symbol of the Eleian victory over the erstwhile lords of the sanctuary.

428 B.C.: The Peloponnesian League assembles at Olympia at the time of the cult festival to discuss further actions in its war

against Athens.

402–401 B.C.: Elis is defeated in its war against Sparta and loses jurisdiction over the Alpheus Valley, but for the time being remains in control of the Zeus sanctuary.

373 B.C.: A heavy earthquake near the coastal town of Helike in the northern Peloponnesus seriously damages the Temple of Zeus. Almost its entire front has to be completely renovated.

c. 365 B.C.: After the Eleians have lost a war, they are forced to cede control of the sanctuary to the Arcadians.

364 B.C.: The cult festival, organized by Arcadia, is disrupted by an Eleian attack. A few years later the Eleians manage to bring the sanctuary and its surrounding land back under their control.

4th to 2nd centuries B.C.: Thanks to donations from private individuals and the activities of various royal families, the sanctuary is extensively expanded (Philippeion, Echo Portico? [unfinished], Leonidaeon, Palaestra, Gymnasion).

146 B.C.: Consul Mummius leads Rome's battles in Greece. He is forced to carry out the Roman senate's decision to destroy Corinth. Personally opposed to that measure, Mummius does raze the city, but not entirely, and subsequently travels through Greece to make donations to the country's large sanctuaries. Olympia is among those places where he has statues erected.

Early 1st century B.C.: To finance Rome's war on Greek soil, Commander Sulla raids treasures from Greece's large sanctuaries, among them, Olympia's. After his victory, Sulla (over the protest of Rome's tax authorities) initiates legal action to obtain compensation for the sanctuaries he has looted.

1st century B.C.: An unidentified patron donates a magnificent entry gate to the area of the *gymnasion*.

31 B.C.: Sea battle near Greece's northwestern coast in the area of Actium. After being in limbo for a prolonged period, Central Greece and the Peloponnesus are finally united as the Roman province of Achaea. The governor resides in Corinth which, with Rome's aid, is splendidly rebuilt and expanded. Roman citizens settle in Patras and Elis. This contributes to a

normalization of Greco-Roman relations, from which Olympia also profits.

Around 1: Augustus' pacification of the Mediterranean lures new benefactors to Olympia (Herod of Judea; Agrippa).

November A.D. 66: On his way to a planned expedition in the Arabian peninsula, Nero stops over in Corinth. On the occasion of the cult festival in nearby Isthmia, he publicly declares the independence of the formerly Roman province of Achaea.

Winter 66–67: Nero travels to the Greek territories that have gained their independence. Following an old tradition, he is honored as a benefactor at all famous places, including Olympia, in joint cult festival celebrations. The emperor puts monies and architects at Olympia's disposal for the purpose of building a clubhouse for the athletes' guilds.

Summer 84: The athletes' clubhouse is completed with the support of Emperor Domitian (inscription on a building).

Summer 85: The athletes gathered in the Zeus sanctuary for the 216th Olympic Games honor the Eleian Lucius Vettulenus Laetus as an eminent benefactor. He had probably established the contacts to the imperial family in Rome that proved so important for Olympia.

Late 1st century: The elegant guesthouse Leonidaeon is remodeled in the contemporary style. Emperor Domitian was probably involved as benefactor.

1st to 3rd centuries: Continuous improvement of the infrastructure of the sanctuary, which enjoys an undiminished stream of visitors (guesthouses; facilities for hygiene, baths, shops).

153: One of the most consequential improvements of the infrastructure is completed: an aqueduct carrying fresh spring water to the sanctuary. It is donated by the wealthy patron Herodes Atticus. In return for being appointed priestess of Demeter, his wife Regilla donates a fountain display.

Late 3rd century: All of the sanctuary's buildings are damaged in a heavy earthquake, but they are immediately repaired. Again new buildings are constructed to accommodate the site's visitors. Apparently this puts so much strain on the bank of the Cladeus that in the following years the sanctuary's western part is repeatedly flooded.

4th century: There are more and more floods of the Alpheus from the fourth century on. An ever-growing layer of alluvial sand accumulates in the western part of the sanctuary. Still, the cult festival had not lost any of its attraction. Athletes from Greek cities continue to travel to the Olympic contests from far away. The as yet last known Olympic victor is a citizen of Athens named Zopyrus. He wins the boxing contest in A.D. 385.

391–92: Emperor Theodosius I orders the old religion's places of worship closed. Evidently the order has little effect, at least in Olympia.

395–97: Alaric's Visigoths advance to the area near Elis.

First half of the 5th century: Emperor Theodosius II reinforces the old order concerning the closing down of the sanctuaries. At a date we cannot exactly determine, the priests of Olympia, too, comply with the order.

III. NONSECULAR POSTLUDE

5th and 6th centuries: Under the supervision of the City of Elis, farmers and tradespeople settle in the area of the former sanctuary. In addition to at least fourteen vintners, there are potters, smiths, and bone cutters. Imported pottery from Asia Minor and northern Africa indicates that the settlers are in contact with these regions. Even after the sanctuary has closed down, Olympia apparently continues to have close trade connections with the Mediterranean.

The settlers convert to Christianity. Shortly after the mid-fifth century they transform one of the great halls from the period of the sanctuary into a Christian church.

The Temple of Zeus and its immediate surroundings are separated from people's homes by a high wall. We are not certain as to the purpose of this little fortress: storage of private property and food supplies in cases of danger, plus temporary lodging of soldiers? Securing of valuable inventory items of the erstwhile sanctuary for use by the emperor—for instance, official melting down of bronze statues? Museum-like preservation of some historical records from the bygone Greco-Roman culture?

c. 470: Gaiseric's Vandals, on their way from Carthage to Epirus, pass Olympia's coast.

522: Major earthquake on the Peloponnesus.

Between 530 and 540: Outbreak of the plague on the Peloponnesus.

551: Another serious earthquake on the Peloponnesus.

c. 580: Avars and Slavs, coming from the north, advance to southern Greece. Numerous inhabitants of the settlement in the former sanctuary leave their homes. Since they first bury their effects, they are apparently not planning to leave for good, but for unknown reasons they do not return.

c. 600: There is another serious flood of the Cladeus. A layer of alluvial sand, up to almost twenty-five inches thick, covers the western part of the settlement.

610–20: The last settlers leave the plane at the foot of the Hill of Cronus.

c. 630: Slavic immigrants settle in the Cladeus Valley, north of the Hill of Cronus. To date, the precise place can still not be located. We do, however, know the necropolis belonging to it, where funerals took place until the late eighth century.

Early 9th century: The plane at the foot of the Hill of Cronus has by now accumulated a thirteen- to sixteen-foot-high layer of alluvial sand from the Cladeus. This is the condition in which the first excavators of Olympia find the area in the nineteenth century.

SELECTED BIBLIOGRAPHY
WITH ANNOTATIONS

There is very little literature in English about Olympia, and much of what exists is out of date. The following titles are recommended:

Coulson, William, and Helmut Kyrieleis, eds. *Proceedings of an International Symposium on the Olympic Games 5–9 September 1988*. Athens, 1992.

Finley, M.I., and H.W. Pleket. *The Olympic Games: The First Thousand Years*. London, 1976.

Kyle, D.G. *Athletes in Ancient Athens*. Leiden, 1987.

Miller, Stephen G. *Arete: Greek Sports from Ancient Sources*. Berkeley, Los Angeles, Oxford, 1991.

Sweet, Waldo E. *Sport and Recreation in Ancient Greece*. New York, Oxford, 1987.

Swaddling, Judith. *The Ancient Olympic Games*. London, 1980.

Tzachou-Alexandri, Olga, ed. *Mind and Body: Athletic Contests in Ancient Greece*. Athens, 1989.

Yalouris, Nicolaos, ed. *The Olympic Games in Ancient Greece*. Athens, 1982.

GENERAL WORKS

The last comprehensive books on the Zeus sanctuary at Olympia were published on the occasion of the Olympic Games in Munich (1972) and Moscow (1980). They are all out of print now, but can still be found in libraries:

Alfred Mallwitz, *Olympia und seine Bauten*, Munich, 1972. An architectural scholar by profession, the author has a clear focus. His extended work at Olympia, which he conducted over many years, allowed Mallwitz to offer pieces of information on architecture and conclusions that had never been available in print elsewhere.

Hans-Volkmar Herrmann, *Olympia: Heiligtum und Wettkampfstätte*, Munich, 1972. This work keys in on the history of art and religion. Scholars will find the section of annotations—which is separate from the text—an additional mine of information. This book, too, profited from the author's direct knowledge gained during many years of excavations.

Joachim Ebert et al., *Olympia von den Anfängen bis Coubertin*, Leipzig, 1980. All too familiar reasons kept these East German authors from examining and analyzing excavated material directly. Instead, they offer a concise summary in the descriptive section of their book. Highly interesting chapters deal with the editor's special field of expertise, the history of sports, and Olympia's later history during the Middle Ages and early modern times.

These three titles with their different focuses complement each other and offer a comprehensive, detailed picture of the sanctuary's significance within the framework of cultural history. From today's point of view, we have to qualify our appraisal: All three books were written before excavations began anew and therefore lack the more recent, fundamental insights into both Olympia's early and late history. In these sections they are in many respects outdated.

PUBLICATIONS ON EXCAVATIONS

Continuous reports on the German Archeological Institute's excavations are offered in the series "Olympia-Berichte" and "Olympische Forschungen," which appear every few years and are published by the German Archeological Institute.

INDIVIDUAL ASPECTS

H. Kyrieleis's excavations, which he resumed in 1986, have provided a new basis for the inquiry into Olympia's beginnings and early history. There are two important articles on the beginning of the cult in the eleventh century B.C. and on the significance of the worship of Pelops: H. Kyrieleis, "Neue

Ausgrabungen in Olympia," in *Antike Welt*, vol. 21 (1990), pp. 177–88; H. Kyrieleis, "Zeus and Pelops in the East Pediment of the Temple of Zeus at Olympia," in *Studies in the History of Art*, Washington, 1996.

The early Olympic cult in the context and as part of the Alpheus Valley is dealt with in U. Sinn, "Das Heiligtum der Artemis Limnatis von Kombothekra," in *Mitteilungen des Deutschen Archäologischen Instituts*, Athenische Abteilung 96, 1981, pp. 25–71.

The way the athletic contests were at first entirely dominated by the oracle is shown in detail in U. Sinn, "Die Stellung der Wettkämpfe im Kult des Zeus Olympios," in *Nikephoros*, vol. 4 (1991), pp. 31–54. An important argument was supplied by A. Mallwitz in his "Cult and Competition Locations at Olympia," in *The Archaeology of the Olympics*, ed. W. J. Raschke, Wisconsin, 1988, pp. 79–109, which contains new observations on the earliest stadium's location and construction dates.

The general assumption that there was a direct connection between the dedication of tripod kettles and the athletic competitions was corrected in M. Maass, "Die geometrischen Dreifüße von Olympia," in *Antike Kunst*, vol. 24 (1981), pp. 6–18.

We owe the radically new assessment of Hera's part in Olympia's cult to A. Mustaka. His surprising but convincing arguments were presented at an international conference in Athens in 1994. Their publication is forthcoming.

That treasuries existed even way back in the seventh century was recognized by H. Philipp. See his "XALKEOI TOIXOI – Eherne Wände," in *Archäologischer Anzeiger*, 1994, pp. 489–98.

The Hippodrome was reconstructed in its actual shape in J. Ebert, "Neues zum Hippodrom und zu den hippischen Konkurrenzen in Olympia," in *Nikephoros*, vol. 2 (1989), pp. 89–108.

A comprehensive view of the architectural history of the Gymnasium and its use aside from the athletic contests is offered in C. Wacker, *Das Gymnasium von Olympia*, Würzburg,

1996.

The existence of a pan-Greek arbitration court at Olympia was proven by P. Siewert in "Eine Bronze-Urkunde mit elischen Urteilen," in *10. Olympiabericht*, Berlin, 1981, pp. 228–48. His argument is complemented by the most recent interpretation of the architectural ornaments at the Temple of Zeus in U. Sinn, "Apollon und die Kentauromachie im Westgiebel des Zeustemples in Olympia: Die Wettkampfstätte als Forum der griechischen Diplomatie nach den Perserkriegen," in *Archäologischer Anzeiger*, 1994, pp. 585–602.

The identification of the Theatron goes back to I. Kontis, *The Sanctuary of Olympia in the Fourth Century B.C.* (Athens, 1958; in modern Greek). W. Koenigs succeeded in dating the embankments of earth and the Echo Portico in his "Stadion III und Echohalle," in *10. Olympia-Bericht*, Berlin (1981), pp. 353–69.

An overview of the history of the sanctuary in late antiquity is offered in U. Sinn, "Pilgrims, Athletes and Christians," in *Proceedings of the XVth International Congress of Classical Archaeology*, Allard Pierson Series 12, Amsterdam, 1998, pp. 32–34.

On the early Byzantine settlement see T. Völling, "Olympia in Late Antiquity," in J. Bintliff, E. Tsougarakis and D. Tsougarakis, eds., *Das slawische Brandgräberfeld von Olympia*, Archäologie in Eurasien 9, Berlin, 2000.

ILLUSTRATION CREDITS

Figs. 1, 3, 4, 5, 10, 12, 18, 20, 24: German Archaeological Institute in Athens.

Figs. 2, 9, 11: Drawings by Jörg Denkinger from copies by the author.

Figs. 6, 7, 8: Martin von Wagner Museum of Würzburg University.

Figs. 13, 14, 15, 16, 17, 19, 21, 22, 23: Author.

PERSONALITIES FROM GREEK AND ROMAN HISTORY

Aelian: Roman scholar and author of a collection of reports of strange events and anecdotes about great men, among other works; lived c. A.D. 170–235.

Aëtion: eminent Greek painter during the mid-fourth century B.C..

Agis II: Spartan king; military commander in battles against Athens and Elis; r. 427–399 B.C.

Agrippa: native of Dalmatia; son-in-law of Augustus, his closest associate and designated successor; 63–12 B.C.

Alexander I: king of the Macedonians, friend of the Greeks; prevailed in obtaining permission for the Macedonians to participate in the Olympic competitions; reigned during the first half of the fifth century B.C.

Alexander III "the Great": king of the Macedonians; r. 336–323 B.C.

Alcibiades: Athenian general and politician with a keen sense of power; lived c. 450–404 B.C.

Antigonus I: Macedonian; associate and, eventually, successor of Alexander the Great; king of Macedonia 306–301 B.C.

Arsinoë II: daughter of Ptolemy I; lived c. 316–270 B.C.; married to her brother Ptolemy II in 278 B.C.; co-regent of Egypt.

Artaxerxes II: powerful Persian king; was forced to fend off an attack by his brother Cyrus in alliance with a Greek army; r. c. 404–c. 360 B.C.

Augustus: Roman statesman, was victorious in 31 B.C. in the Battle of Actium, which decided the Roman civil war; founder of the Roman Empire; r. 27 B.C.–A.D. 14.

Cassius Dio: Greek historian from Bithynia; lived c. A.D. 163–230; from A.D. 180 government official in Rome.

Cluvius Rufus: Roman historian of the first century A.D.; probably an associate of Emperor Nero; made a political about-face after Nero's death.

Diodorus: Greek historian from Sicily; lived in the first century A.D.

Diogenes: Greek philosopher from Sinope; most prominent representative of Cynicism; lived in the fourth century B.C.

Diogenes Laërtius: Greek writer of the third century A.D.; voluminous, but uncritical, collection containing the views of older philosophical movements and their representatives.

Domitian: Roman emperor; r. A.D. 81–96.

Euripides: eminent Greek playwright; lived c. 485–406 B.C.

Fabius Rusticus: Roman historian of the first century A.D.; sympathizer of Seneca and, therefore, fierce adversary of Emperor Nero.

Germanicus: adopted son of Roman Emperor Tiberius; lived 15 B.C.–19 A.D.; winner of the chariot race at Olympia in A.D. 17.

Gorgias: eminent Greek teacher of rhetoric; lived between 480 and 380 B.C.; festival speeches at Olympia and Delphi.

Herodes Atticus: Greek philosopher and politician; spent his immense riches on the preservation of his homeland's cultural heritage; married to the Roman Regilla; lived A.D. 101–177.

Herod I, called "the Great": king of Judea; consolidated his power through strict loyalty to Rome; lived c. 73–4 B.C.

Herodotus: Greek historian from Halicarnassus; lived c. 484–430 B.C.

Hippias: Greek scholar from Elis; wrote his main works in the late fifth century B.C.

Isocrates: eminent Greek orator from Athens; lived 436–338 B.C.

Leonidas: king in Sparta, r. 488–480 B.C.; sacrificed himself in the battle against the Persians of 480 B.C.

Leonides of Naxos: Greek architect of the fourth century B.C.

Lucian: native of Syria; scholar and satirist writing in Greek; visited Olympia in A.D. 165; lived. c. A.D. 120–180.

Lysias: eminent Greek orator from Athens; lived c. 445–380 B.C.

Marc Antony: Roman general and politician; emulated the style of Greek rulers; his liaison with Cleopatra in Alexandria must also be seen in this context; lived 82–30 B.C.

Miltiades: Athenian statesman; military commander in the Battle of Marathon in 490 B.C.; lived c. 550–488 B.C.

Mummius: Roman general of the second century B.C.; as Roman consul, defeated Central and Southern Greece; personally, was favorably inclined toward Greek culture.

Nero: Roman emperor; after his early education in the ancient Roman spirit by Seneca, he developed a passion for Greek culture; r. A.D. 54–68.

Nicaenetus: Greek poet from Samos; lived and worked during the third or second century B.C.

Pausanias: Greek born in Asia Minor; author of a Greek cultural history, written in the style of a fictitious Greek travelogue; lived c. A.D. 115–180.

Peregrinus: Greek itinerary philosopher of Cynicism; dramatically staged suicide at Olympia in A.D. 165.

Phidias: eminent Athenian sculptor; worked in close cooperation with Pericles on the reconstruction of the Acropolis in Athens; lived 495–430 B.C.

Philip II: Macedonian king; r. 359–336 B.C.; father and predecessor of Alexander the Great.

Pindar: Greek poet from Thebes in Boeotia, lived 522–438 B.C.

Plato: eminent Greek philosopher; 427–347 B.C.; developed detailed ideas on the ideal state in intense discussions with his pupils.

Pliny the Older: Roman civil servant and writer; b. A.D. 23 or 24, d. during an eruption of Mt. Vesuvius in A.D. 79.

Plutarch: Greek philosopher from Chaeroneia in Boeotia; held positions in the local administration, priest in Delphi; lived c. A.D. 50–120.

Polydamas: heavy athlete from Thessalia, won the pankration at Olympia in 408 B.C.

Ptolemy I: Macedonian follower of Alexander the Great; founder of the Hellenized royal dynasty in Egypt, r. 305–283 B.C.

Ptolemy II: co-regent and successor of Ptolemy I, r. 285–246 B.C.

Regilla: noble Roman woman; married to Herodes Atticus.

Socrates: Greek philosopher from Athens; b. 469 B.C., was sentenced to death in 399 B.C. for his views which were allegedly incompatible with the religious norms of his time.

Strabo: Greek geographer and historian from Pontus; lived c. 64 B.C.–A.D. 19.

Suetonius: Roman aristocrat with ambitions as a writer, biographer of eminent persons; lived c. A.D. 70–140.

Sulla: Roman statesman and general; lived 138–78 B.C.

Telesphorus: member of the Macedonian aristocracy; lived in the second half of the fourth century B.C.

Thales: Greek philosopher from Milet, one of the "Seven Sages"; lived in the first half of the sixth century B.C.

Theagenes: boxer from Thasos, Olympic champion in 476 and 472 B.C.

Themistocles: Athenian statesman; lived c. 525–460 B.C.; military commander in the Battle of Plataea.

Theodosius I, called "the Great": Roman emperor; r. A.D. 379–395.

Theodosius II: Roman emperor, r. A.D. 402–450 in Constantinople.

Thucydides: Greek historian from Athens; lived c. 460–400 B.C.

Tiberius: Roman emperor, r. A.D. 14–37.

Tyrtaeus: Greek poet from Milet, later moved to Sparta; lived in the seventh century B.C.

Vettuleni: old aristocratic family from Rome, living as merchants in various regions in Greece from the first century B.C. on.

Vitruvius: Roman architect and engineer; lived around the time of Christ.

Xenophanes: poet and philosopher from Colophon near Ephesus; lived c. 545–470 B.C.

Xenophon: philosopher and historian from Athens; lived c. 430–355 B.C.

Zopyrus: boxer from Athens; last known Olympic champion, in A.D. 385, in boxing.

NAMES IN GREEK MYTHS
AND LEGENDS

Agamemnon: prince of Mycenae.

Aphrodite: in early Greek mythology, goddess of navigation, of war and fertility; later on mainly goddess of love.

Apollo: in early Greek mythology, as Apollo Pyktes; represented as a boxer, he was a role model for athletes; in Olympia, founder of the local oracle

Artemis: goddess of fertile land; protector of women and girls.

Athena: in early Greek mythology, goddess of battle; protector of many mythic heroes, for instance, Hercules.

Athena Parthenus

Augeas : prince in Elis, owner of large herds of cattle.

Centaurs: half human, half horse-like inhabitants of the Pelion mountains in Thessalia; on the one hand they embody unbridled ferocity, but on the other wise Chiron, educator of the hero Achilles, is a centaur as well.

Chamyne: surname of Demeter.

Clytius, Clytiads: after the Iamids, second Olympian family of seers.

Demeter: goddess of fertile land.

Eileithyia: divine midwife.

Euadne: daughter of an Arcadian prince.

Gaia: giver of the life springing from the earth.

Hera: wife, but also rival of Zeus.

Hercules: national hero especially of the Dorian Greeks living on the Peloponnesus; from the sixth century B.C. he increasingly took over the role of Apollo as patron of the athletes.

Hestia: goddess of the holy hearth; her monuments are typically associated with the seat of political power in the Prytaneion.

Homer: legendary author of the *Iliad* and the *Odyssey*; his name stands for an entire group of individual, anonymous poets.

Iamus, Iamids: hereditary seers in the service of the Olympian oracle; documented through inscriptions until the third century A.D.

Iphitus: legendary prince of Elis.

Isis: ancient Egyptian goddess, popular in Greece from the fourth century B.C. on as a goddess related to Demeter; a mystery cult was founded around her.

Lapiths: inhabitants of Thessalia.

Lycurgus: legendary Spartan lawgiver.

Mithras: Indo-Iranian god who was established particularly among Roman merchants and soldiers in the western Mediterranean from the first century on.

Nestor: prince of Pylos; oldest and most circumspect military commander before Troy.

Nike: in Olympia, personification of victory in war as granted by Zeus.

Nymphs: divine female creatures in nature.

Peirithous: prince of the Lapiths.

Pelops: hailing from Asia Minor, he gained control of the Alpheus Valley after winning a chariot race with the aid of Poseidon.

Poseidon: on the Peloponnesus—as "shaker of the earth"—decidedly a land god; protector of horses; supporter of Pelops.

Theseus: the Athenian-Ionian equivalent of the Dorian hero Hercules.

INDEX OF SUBJECTS AND PLACES

147